Illustrator® 9
Visual Insight

T. Michael Clark

The Coriolis Group, LLC
14455 North Hayden Road
Suite 220
Scottsdale, Arizona 85260

(480) 483-0192
FAX: (480) 483-0193
www.coriolis.com

Library of Congress Cataloging-in-Publication Data
Clark, T. Michael.
Illustrator 9 visual insight/ by T. Michael Clark.
  p. cm
  Includes index.
  ISBN 1-5710-749-3
    1. Computer graphics. 2. Adobe Illustrator
(computer file) I. Title.
T385.C5235 2000
006.6'869--dc21   00-050884
                     CIP

President, CEO
Keith Weiskamp

Publisher
Steve Sayre

Acquisitions Editor
Beth Kohler

Development Editor
Michelle Stroup

Product Marketing Manager
Patricia Davenport

Project Editor
Sally M. Scott

Technical Reviewer
Jim Alley

Production Coordinator
Meg E. Turecek

Cover Designer
Jody Winkler

Layout Designer
April Nielsen

Printed in the United States of America
10 9 8 7 6 5 4 3 2 1

Other Titles for the Creative Professional

I'd like to dedicate this book to my lovely and loving wife, Pamela.

About the Author

T. Michael Clark is the author of several prominent books on computer imaging software. Titles include *Photoshop 5 Filters f/x and Design* (The Coriolis Group, 1999), *Illustrator 8 f/x and Design* (The Coriolis Group, 1999, with Sherry London), *Teach Yourself Photoshop 5 in 21 Days*, *Teach Yourself Paint Shop Pro 7 in 24 Hours*, and *Paint Shop Pro Web Techniques*. Michael's clear, concise teaching style has won much acclaim, and he is very pleased to be able to share his love of the Internet with his many readers.

An artist practically from birth, freelance photographer, computer consultant, certified programmer-analyst, and full-time author, Michael owns and operates GrafX Design (**www.grafx-design.com**), a Web site that offers online tutorials, product reviews, and a host of lessons on computer-imaging topics. He teaches Web-site design, Web graphics, and Web technician courses at the college level, both on site at several colleges and online. He welcomes email from his readers and can be reached at **tmc@grafx-design.com**.

Acknowledgments

I'd like to thank the following people and companies for their help in putting this book together. Without each and every one of them (and more whom no doubt I've forgotten to mention), this book would not have been possible.

My agent, Margot Maley Hutchison, and her stand-in, Wendy Dietrich.

The amazing staff at The Coriolis Group, including, but not limited to: Beth Kohler, Michelle Stroup, and Sally Scott.

The technical editor, Jim Alley, for helping to make sure that everything worked properly.

The software companies, for making such fun products: Adobe, for creating Illustrator; Nakae Software Development and CValley, Inc, for creating FILTERiT (a great Illustrator plug-in); and Ambrosia Software, for creating Snapz Pro^2, which I used to create the Mac screenshots.

A special thanks goes to my model, Melanie Besner.

Last, but certainly not least, I'd like to thank you, the reader, and everyone who surfs by GrafX Design. It's all of you who spur me on to new heights with the software I use on a daily basis, and it's all of you who keep me going with your email questions and responses.

—*T. Michael Clark*

Contents at a Glance

Table of Contents

Introduction

I love computers and digital graphics software. And since you're holding this book in your hands, I suspect that you do, too. One of the fun things about computers and digital graphics software is that they are constantly changing. Unfortunately, this can also be a problem when you're trying to keep up with the constant changes. Whether you're a novice or an experienced user quickly trying to learn the basics of Illustrator 9, I believe this book will be a big help to you.

About Illustrator 9

Illustrator 9 is a powerful tool that enables people, even graphically challenged ones who claim that they "can't draw a straight line," to create amazing artwork. Whether you're trying to design a new business card, spiff up your company's letterhead, design a poster, create a logo for your Web page, or build a new interface for your Web site, you'll find Illustrator is exactly the right tool for the job.

As powerful as it is, however, Illustrator is not a difficult tool to learn to use. I feel that, with the help of this book, anyone should be able to create original digital artwork they can be proud of. All it will take is some time and effort on your part.

This Book's Structure

This book is divided into two sections: The first part, which contains Chapters 1 through 10, focuses primarily on the basics of the program. It introduces you to Illustrator's tools and its fundamental techniques and procedures, beginning with the essentials and moving on to introduce increasingly advanced topics and materials. Simply put, you'll learn how Illustrator works. You'll be introduced to the tools, palettes, and menus in a visual fashion. Being a visual artist, or even just a budding one, you'll appreciate how easy it is to follow along.

The second part, which contains Chapters 11 through 14, shows you how to use those tools, techniques, and procedures to create your own distinctive designs. Using the knowledge you've gained from the first section of the book, these chapters will take you step by step through a number of hands-on projects intended to show you how to create your own artwork.

The books in the Visual Insight series are formatted in such a way as to lead you visually through the software program, with the added benefit of enabling you to flip through the pages and see at a glance the tasks that can be accomplished and how to accomplish them in a quick and easy fashion.

Who This Book Is For

This book is intended for a variety of users with a variety of skill levels. You can use this book in a number of ways depending on your experience with Illustrator and digital graphics.

- If you're a new user, you may want to start with the first chapter and work your way through the entire book.

- If you've used Illustrator before, you may want to skim through the first part, paying attention to those areas that interest you or those that cover material you're not yet familiar with, before you turn to the projects in the second part.

- If you're familiar with digital graphics but are new to Illustrator and vector-based graphics, this book will serve as a good introduction to both topics.

Whatever your skill level, I encourage you to work through the book while experimenting with the different aspects of Illustrator as you go. Illustrator is a great program that has a lot to offer everyone.

And as in any graphics program, usually a number of methods can be used to execute any given task; by adding your own creative modifications to the techniques and projects in this book, you may come up with something truly amazing.

Part I
Techniques and Tasks

Chapter 1
Learning the Interface

- Learn to navigate the menus

- Discover the Toolbox and palettes

- Customize your workspace

- Learn about the Help system

Menus, Toolboxes, and Palettes

Illustrator, like most of today's computer applications, runs as a GUI (Graphical User Interface) application. What this means is that all of the features and functions are accessible from the screen using a mouse, a tablet, or keyboard shortcuts. It also means that many of the tools are presented to you, the user, in the form of menus, toolboxes, and palettes.

Exploring the Interface

After loading Illustrator (by choosing its entry from the Start|Programs menu if you're running Windows, or by double-clicking its icon if you're using a Mac), you'll see a start-up screen where you'll see a menu across the top, a toolbox on the left side of the screen and a series of palettes along the right. You'll see exactly the same layout on a Mac as on a PC, but the screen background will be visible behind Illustrator's components. Looking at the Illustrator screen, you'll notice the following components:

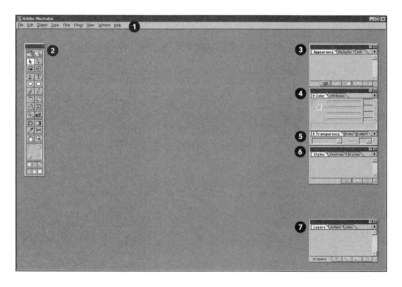

1. The Menu Bar

2. The Toolbox

3. The Appearance, Navigator, and Info palettes

4. The Color and Attributes palettes

5. The Transparency, Stroke, and Gradient palettes

6. The Styles, Swatches, and Brushes palettes

7. The Layers, Actions, and Links palettes

More palettes exist, but they are not visible on the default screen. We'll explore these other palettes later in the chapter.

Accessing Menu Choices

Many of Illustrator's functions can be accessed from the pull-down menus that appear when you click on the menu bar located across the top of the screen. Slide the mouse pointer along the menu bar to see the various available drop-down menus. For example, to create a new file, choose File from the menu bar, and then choose New from the pull-down menu.

You may notice that some of the menu choices are grayed-out. This is because the menus are context sensitive. This means that these choices are not available within this particular context. For example, the Save choice is not available because there is no open file yet.

Ellipses

Another thing you might notice is that some menu choices have extra symbols after their names. These symbols—the ellipses and the small black arrow—are associated with many menu choices in Illustrator. The ellipses mean there is a dialog box associated with the menu choice. For example, if you choose "New" under the File menu, you'll be presented with the New Document dialog box.

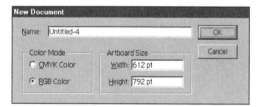

Small Black Arrows

The small black arrow signifies that there are sub-menus available under the choice associated with the arrow. For example, under the Document Color Mode choice is a submenu that lets you choose from the two color modes, CMYK Color and RGB Color. You can use this menu to change the file's color mode quickly.

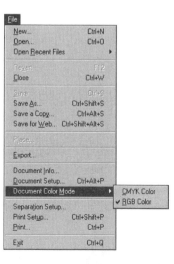

Discovering the Tools in the Toolbox

All of the tools you'll use in the creation of your Illustrator images are accessible via the Toolbox.

The Toolbox is, by default, located along the left-hand side of the screen.

Connecting to Adobe Online

At the top of the Toolbox is the Illustrator logo. Clicking on this brings up a dialog box that offers several ways to connect to Adobe Online (note that your computer must be equipped with some way to access the Internet).

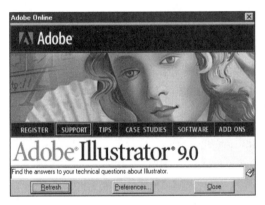

You can receive help on the following subjects from this dialog box:

- Register
- Support
- Tips
- Case Studies
- Software
- Add-ons

Clicking on any of these choices will take you to the appropriate Web page at Adobe.

Toolbox Tools

In the Toolbox, you'll find the following tools. (Note that the tools can be selected by clicking on the icon [left-clicking if you're using a PC] or by selecting the associated keyboard shortcut, which I'll show in parentheses.) The first eleven tools listed here are on the left side of the Toolbox, and the second half of the list are on the right side.

1. Selection tool (V)

2. Lasso tool (Y)

3. Pen tool (P)

4. Ellipse tool (L)

5. Paintbrush tool (B)

6. Rotate tool (R)

7. Reflect tool (O)

8. Blend tool (W)

9. Gradient Mesh tool (U)

10. Eyedropper tool (I)

11. Hand tool (H)

12. Direct Selection tool (A)

13. Direct Select Lasso tool (Q)

14. Type tool (T)

15. Rectangle tool (M)

16. Pencil tool (N)

17. Scale tool (S)

18. Free Transform tool (E)

19. Column Graph tool (J)

20. Gradient tool (G)

21. Scissors tool (C)

22. Zoom tool (Z)

The Fill and Stroke Icons

Below the tools in the Toolbox, you'll find the Fill and Stroke icons. You'll see a couple of large squares along with two smaller icons in the upper-right and lower-left corners. The large icon towards the upper left indicates the current fill color and the other large icon indicates the current stroke (outline). Clicking on either of these will bring the icon forward and enable you to change the color (and/or gradient in the case of the fill).

The small icons in the corners each have a special purpose: the one in the upper-right corner enables you to quickly swap the properties of the fill and stroke (X), and the other enables you to quickly set the default white fill and black fill (D).

Editing and Screen View Modes

Below the fill and stroke icons are two more rows of small icons.

The first row lets you quickly set the most recently chosen color (<) and gradient (>) or set the fill or stroke to none (/).

The second, and last, row of icons enables you to set the Screen Mode. You can choose from Standard Screen Mode (F), Full Screen Mode with Menu Bar (F), and Full Screen Mode (F). The fact that all three choices have the same keyboard shortcut is not a typo. Pressing the "F" key will cycle you through the three choices.

Flyout Menus

You may have noticed that some of the icons in the Toolbox have small (very small) black arrows in their lower-right corners. These arrows indicate that there are flyout menus available under these particular icons.

You'll notice that these tools form similar groups, for the most part. We'll explore many of these tools throughout the remainder of this book.

Direct Selection Tool Flyout Menu

Under the Direct Selection tool, you'll find:

- Group Selection tool (+)

Pen Tool Flyout Menu

Under the Pen tool, you'll find:

- Add Anchor Point tool (+)
- Delete Anchor Point tool (-)
- Convert Anchor Point tool (Shift C)

Type Tool Flyout Menu

Under the Type tool, you'll find:

- Area Type tool
- Path Type tool
- Vertical Type tool
- Vertical Area Type tool
- Vertical Path Type tool

Ellipse Tool Flyout Menu

Under the Ellipse tool, you'll find:

- Polygon tool
- Star tool
- Spiral tool

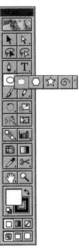

Rectangle Tool Flyout Menu

Under the Rectangle tool, you'll find:

- Rounded Rectangle tool

Pencil Tool Flyout Menu

Under the Pencil tool, you'll find:

- Smooth tool

- Erase tool

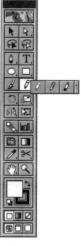

Rotate Tool Flyout Menu

Under the Rotate tool, you'll find:

- Twirl tool

Scale Tool Flyout Menu

Under the Scale tool, you'll find:

- Reshape tool

Reflect Tool Flyout Menu

Under the Reflect tool, you'll find:

- Shear tool

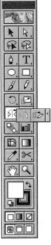

Blend Tool Flyout Menu

Under the Blend tool, you'll find:

- Auto Trace tool

Column Graph Tool Flyout Menu

Under the Column Graph tool, you'll find:

- Stacked Column Graph tool

- Bar Graph tool

- Stacked Bar Graph tool

- Line Graph tool

- Area Graph tool

- Scatter Graph tool

- Pie Graph tool

- Radar Graph tool

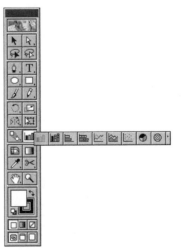

Eyedropper Tool Flyout Menu

Under the Eyedropper tool, you'll find:

- Paint Bucket tool

Scissors Tool Flyout Menu

Under the Scissors tool, you'll find:

- Knife tool

Hand Tool Flyout Menu

Under the Hand tool, you'll find:

- Page tool

- Measure tool

Understanding the Palettes

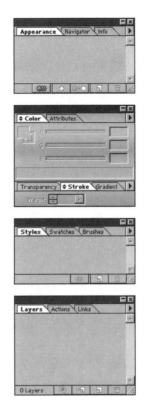

The palettes contain options and settings you can apply to the objects you draw with Illustrator.

When you first open Illustrator, you'll see four palettes down the right-hand side of the screen, each of which can hold several other palettes. These can be accessed via the tabs along the top of each palette. You can also show or hide the various palettes, including those not visible on the screen at all, by making choices from the Window menu.

For example, you can choose Window|Show Navigator, to show the Navigator palette. Note that choosing to hide the only palette showing in a set of palettes in the menu will close that particular palette window.

You can actually close (or hide), and reopen (or show), all of the palettes by pressing the Tab key. This key acts as a toggle hiding/showing the palettes and the Toolbox.

Navigating the Palettes

Navigating through the palettes is quite easy. To show one of the underlying palettes, simply click on the tab of the palette you wish to access. If you can't immediately find the palette you're looking for, choose Window from the menu and look down the list for available palettes. The latter method can be used to open palettes that don't appear on your screen.

Accessing Additional Palette Options

Additional options are available. Sometimes the only option is to show you the palette's other options. You can find these options by clicking the small black triangular arrow in the lower-right corner of each palette.

Choosing Show Options will expand the palette, showing you all the available options in that particular palette.

Customizing Your Workspace

Expanding and shrinking palettes can cause some havoc with the layout of your screen. Fortunately, it's quite easy to customize your workspace in Illustrator. It's possible to work with several screen modes, and you can toggle on and off the palettes and toolbox using the Tab key.

You can actually "tear-off" palettes and rejoin them with the same, or other, sets by simply clicking and dragging the tab for the palette you wish to tear off. For example, you might wish to make the Transparency palette a separate palette from the others it usually resides with.

Rejoining the palette is just as simple. To re-place the Transparency palette, simply click on its tab and drag and drop it onto the palette you removed it from.

Arranging the palettes in your workspace is even easier. To move any set of palettes, simply grab the palette by its title bar and drag it wherever you want it. Once you've moved one set, you can easily line up all the others since they will automatically "snap-to" others as you move them close to each other.

Using these methods, you can arrange the palettes and rearrange your workspace as your working conditions dictate.

Accessing Other Palettes

As mentioned earlier, some palettes are not immediately visible when you first open Illustrator. To bring these palettes, such as the Pathfinder palette, into view, choose Window| Show Pathfinder.

This same method can be used to open and show the different libraries, such as the various Brush Libraries and Style Libraries.

The Help System

Even professionals need help once in a while, perhaps just to reacquaint themselves with a seldom-used tool. When this happens, the manual may be nowhere to be found. That's where the online help comes in handy.

When you invoke the Help command via the Help menu, Illustrator will bring up the Illustrator Help system via your default Web browser. Since most users are at least somewhat familiar with a Web browser's interface, it should be fairly simple to navigate through the Help system.

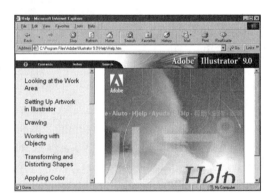

Contents, Index, and Search Tabs

Along the top, on the left, you'll find a small question mark icon. Clicking on it will give you help with the Help system.

Next to the question mark you'll find the Contents, Index, and Search tabs. Selecting any of these will give you help in different ways. The initial setting, Contents, presents you with a list of topics that help you get started with Illustrator. You'll find all the basic topics—from Looking at the Work Area and Drawing to Shortcuts—covered in this area.

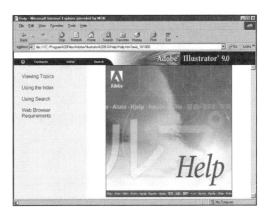

Accessing the Indexed Help

Selecting the Index tab will present you with the alphabet in the upper-left corner. Clicking a letter will give you a list of topics below the alphabet, starting with the letter you selected.

To view one of the topics, simply click the numeral beside the topic. This will provide you with a fairly in-depth look at the topic you selected.

Searching the Help System

More advanced users will prefer to use the Search feature of the Help system. Clicking on the Search tab will bring up a small window within the browser where you can enter a search word.

Reading a Help Entry

Entering a search term and pressing Enter or clicking on Search will present you with a listing, below the area where you entered the search term, of all the help pages that contain the search word. Simply click on the number next to the entry you want to access to see that entry's page.

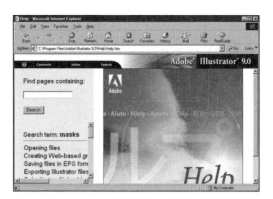

Chapter 2
Getting Started

- Prepare to create your first image

- Save your images

- Move from vectors to bitmaps

- Export your images

- Import artwork

- Use Illustrator with other programs

Running Illustrator

Adobe's products are very similar across platforms. That is, they operate and appear the same way on both a Mac and a PC. One of the very few differences with Adobe products between the two platforms is how you open, or start, the programs.

To open Illustrator on a Mac, use the Apple menu or double-click on the program's icon. On a PC, choose Start|Programs|Adobe Illustrator 9.0 or double-click on the program's icon.

The Splash Screen

As the program loads, you'll see the splash screen. This gives you some info about the program, including which version you're running.

On a PC, you can see the splash screen again by choosing Help|About Illustrator. If you hold down the ALT key (Option key on a Mac) while doing so, you'll see one of the hidden "Easter Eggs." This particular hidden treasure is a different splash screen inspired by Matisse. On a Mac, look under the Apple menu and choose "About Illustrator."

Creating Your First Image

Before you do anything with Illustrator, you'll want to create, or open, a new file where you can create your masterpiece.

To open a new file, choose File|New.

Naming Your New File

Choosing File|New will open the New Document dialog box. You'll notice that the Name: area is highlighted. You can enter a name for your image here.

Choosing a Color Mode

After choosing a title for your artwork, you will need to set the color mode. You can choose from either CMYK Color or RGB Color. If you will be printing the image on a high-end printer or you need to create color separations for printing, choose CMYK. If the final artwork is intended to be seen on a computer screen (on the Web, for example), choose RGB Color.

You can change from one color mode to another after you've created an image. Doing so is not recommended, though, as there may be some color shifting as you change from one mode to the other. This is due to the fact that fewer colors are available in CMYK than in RGB.

Setting the Artboard Size

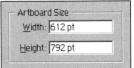

The last thing you need to set is the Artboard Size, although you can often use just the default setting. The artboard size uses the scale you set in the preferences settings (choose Edit|Preferences|Units & Undo). By default, the scale is measured in "pt" for points.

You can set both the Width and the Height, and you do so by highlighting the current choices and entering new values.

Saving Your Image

As you create and work on your illustration, you'll want to save it. To do so, choose File|Save.

In the Save dialog box, browse to the folder where you want to store the file, enter the name you want to call the file, and choose a file type (format on a Mac). You can choose from Adobe PDF (PDF), Illustrator (AI), or Illustrator EPS (EPS). To use any other file type, you'll have to export the image.

Choosing the Compatibility

When you click on Save, you'll see another dialog box where you can set several options.

First, you should choose the Compatibility. This enables you to save the file with backwards compatibility, so that it can be opened by users of older versions of Illustrator.

Illustrator 8 is capable of opening Illustrator 9 files. This can cause problems, however, because Illustrator 8 is not capable of displaying some of the enhancements in Illustrator 9 files. There is a solution, though. Adobe has made available a plug-in for Illustrator 8. This is freely available from the Adobe Web site at www .adobe.com

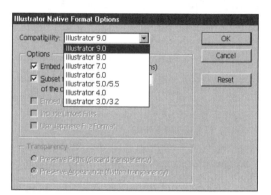

Embedding Fonts and Color Profiles

After choosing the version compatibility, you can choose from the many other options available.

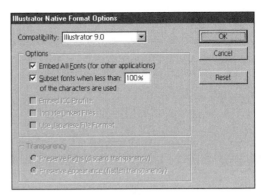

For example, you can choose how to embed fonts. You can choose to embed all fonts, or only subset them. Subsetting a font will help reduce the size of the resulting file.

You can also save ICC profiles (color information), include linked files (which will increase the size of your files), and use Japanese file format. These choices will be grayed-out unless they're appropriate for the image you're saving.

You can also choose whether to discard the transparency information or save it.

Note that the transparency options will be available only if you choose to save the file in a legacy (i.e., older than version 9) format.

Saving PDF Files

Saving as a PDF file has its own set of options.

You can quickly set the Default Option setting, a Screen Optimized setting, or a Custom setting. Choosing the Default or Screen Optimized setting will change the settings for the File Compression and the Options. The Default Option sets the Preserve Illustrator Editing Capabilities and the Generate Thumbnails, while the Screen Optimized setting removes these. You can also choose Custom and set these options to whatever you like.

Setting PDF File Compatibility

The General setting enables you to set the File Compatibility and the Options.

Setting PDF File Compression

You can also set the compression options by selecting Compression from the pull-down menu.

Setting the Compression of Images

After choosing the Compression option, you can set the compression of various types of bitmap images. To save time and get the best settings, you can choose Default|Screen Optimized or Default|Custom from the Options Set menu.

You can get the best results and smallest file sizes by choosing the right compression settings. Choose ZIP for images with large areas of similar colors and JPEG for real-world images such as embedded photographs.

Saving EPS Files

The last file type for saving a file is EPS. EPS files save most of the attributes of the original Illustrator file and can be reopened and edited with Illustrator.

You can set the following options when saving as an EPS file:

- *Compatibility*—Choose from a version of Illustrator to keep the file's backward compatibility.

- *Preview*—Choose a preview file type.

You can also decide to include linked files, thumbnails, or fonts; whether to use the Japanese file format; and which Postscript level to use.

Finally, you can choose to discard or preserve any transparency. (Note that preserving any transparencies you've created will require that the object be converted to bitmap.)

Moving from Vectors to Bitmaps and More

At some point, you'll most likely need to convert your vector image to bitmap. For example, you might want to export your image to a Web-ready GIF or JPEG file. You have many options available for doing so. You might also want to export an Illustrator file to the popular Flash format (SWF). This is easily accomplished using the Export command.

Exporting to Different File Formats

To export your artwork, choose File|Export. Doing so will bring up the Export dialog box.

The Export Dialog Box

From within the Export dialog box, you can name your file and choose from a fairly comprehensive list of file types. Some of these types are meaningful only if you have the appropriate software, such as AutoCAD; you need to open your Illustrator artwork in one of these programs.

You may find a couple of choices useful. You can export images for the Web in JPEG, SVG, and Flash format, and you can export images in PSD (the native Photoshop file format) format if you want to open them in Photoshop.

Exporting JPEG Files

You can export files in the JPEG format to use on your Web pages by choosing Export and then choosing JPEG from the pull-down menu.

Enter a name for your file and click on Save to bring up the JPEG Options dialog box.

Setting the JPEG Quality

Set the Quality (higher numbers are better but create a larger file), the Color Model (it's usually best to stick with RGB for onscreen images), the Format (the default Baseline [Standard] is best to ensure compatibility with all Web browsers), and the Resolution (stick with 72 dpi for Web-based images). You can also choose whether your artwork should be anti-aliased (having the edges smoothed) and whether you want to create an image map (either client-side or server-side).

Exporting Scalable (SVG) Files

Scalable Vector Graphics (SVG) is a new file format for the Web. This is an exciting addition for Web designers since the format creates small, scalable vector files that can be viewed directly in most Web browsers through the use of a free plug-in. This is available at Adobe's Web site, www .adobe.com

To export an image as SVG, choose File|Export and set the Save As Type to SVG.

You can choose between compressed and regular SVG options. I recommend you try both and see which works best for you and your application.

Setting the SVG Options

Give the file a name and click on Save to bring up the SVG Options dialog box.

From among other options, you can choose to Subset and Embed the fonts you've used in your image.

Exporting Flash Movies (SWF) Files

Illustrator 9 is capable of exporting files that can be opened as movie files in Flash format. This works best if you create a multi-layered image and export the layers as separate frames that can be used in a Flash movie.

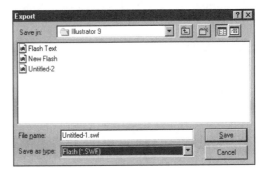

Setting Flash (SWF) Options

To create an image that can be exported as a Flash movie, create a multi-layered image. With the image created, choose File|Export, and choose SWF from the pull-down menu.

Enter a name for your file and click on Save to bring up the Flash (SWF) Format Options dialog box. To save the layers as separate frames for your movie, choose AI Layers To SWF Frames, under the Export As pull-down menu.

More Flash Options

You can set several other options. You can set the Frame Rate in number of frames per second (fps) and choose to Auto-Create Symbols. You can also make the file Read Only so it can't be opened and edited in Flash. Doing so will prevent others from editing your movie file. You can also choose to crop the movie to the size of the artboard.

Another option allows you to set the Curve Quality. This will determine the smoothness of the curves in the resulting Flash file. Smoother curves (higher settings) will increase the file size.

Exporting Photoshop 5 (PSD) Files

Moving files back and forth between Photoshop and Illustrator is common, and now, with Illustrator 9, even easier. For example, you can export Illustrator files to Photoshop and still be able to edit the type.

Setting Photoshop File Options

To export an Illustrator file to Photoshop, choose File|Export and set the Save As Type to Photoshop 5 (PSD). Name your file and click on Save to bring up the Photoshop Options dialog box.

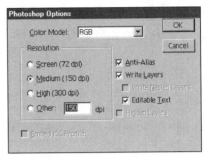

Set the Color Mode to either RGB or CMYK and select a Resolution depending on the intended use of the final image. If you want soft edges, leave the Anti-Alias option on.

You should also leave the Write Layers option turned on so that all Illustrator layers will be written to the Photoshop file. If you want the type from the Illustrator file to be editable in the resulting Photoshop file, check that option.

Although the type will be editable, when exported to Photoshop it may lose some of its attributes. For example, type that has a stroke as well as a fill will lose the stroke if you attempt to edit it in Photoshop.

Saving Images for the Web

Illustrator 9 gives you the ability to export images directly as Web-ready GIF and JPEG files. To export an image you've created in Illustrator, simply choose File|Save For Web. This will bring up the Save For Web dialog box.

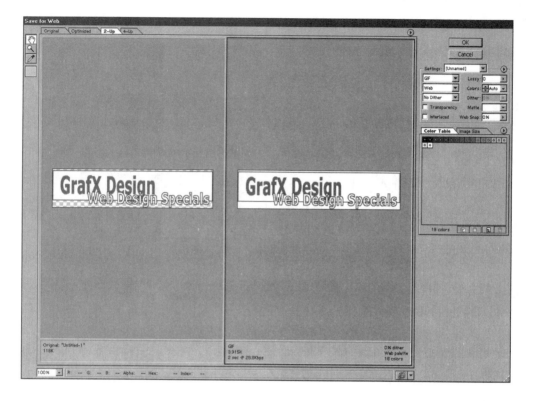

You can choose from a number of different views. The default is to show the original image and the optimized image in a "2-Up" side-by-side view. You can also see the Original, Optimized, or 4-Up view (which allows for four different views using different types and settings). Being able to see the original and the optimized files together in real-time as you change various settings helps in balancing compression with quality.

Choosing the Settings

If you're not familiar with Web graphics, you can choose from a variety of preset GIF and JPEG settings. Keep in mind that none of these settings will affect your original artwork in any way until you save the file with these new settings. This makes it easy to play with the settings to come up with a good-quality compressed image for your Web pages.

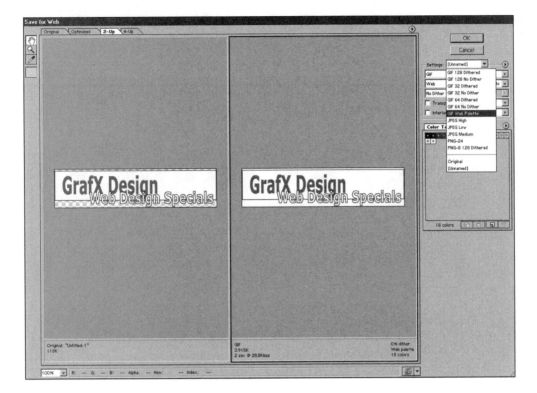

GIF

The GIF file format is great for images that contain large areas of similar color. This is also a good compression scheme if you have an image, such as an illustration, made up of a limited number of colors. After choosing the GIF option, you can choose the palette, set the number of colors, resize the image, and find out how long the image will take to download.

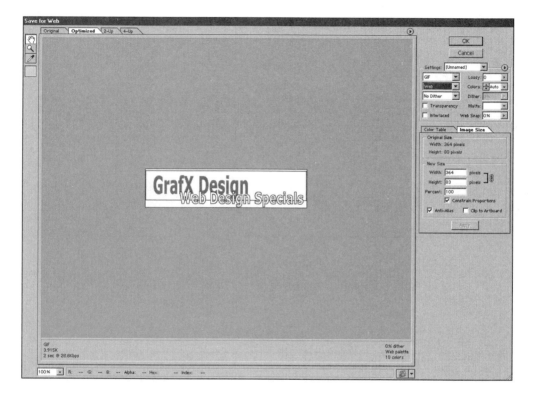

JPEG

JPEG is a good format for real-world images such as photographs and images with soft blends (such as shadows) and gradients. After choosing the JPEG option, you can set the level of compression, whether or not to optimize the JPEG file, whether the Progressive option should be used, and if the image should be blurred slightly to reduce JPEG artifacts.

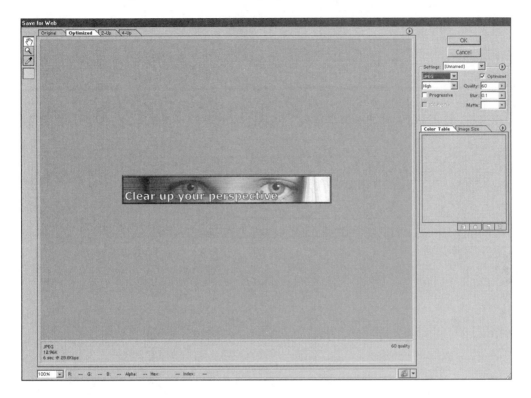

Selecting a Browser for Web Preview

You can get an idea of what your resulting Web-ready GIF or JPEG will look like in a Web browser by clicking on the small browser icon located in the lower-right corner of the Save For Web window. You can also choose a browser by clicking on the small arrow to the right of the browser icon.

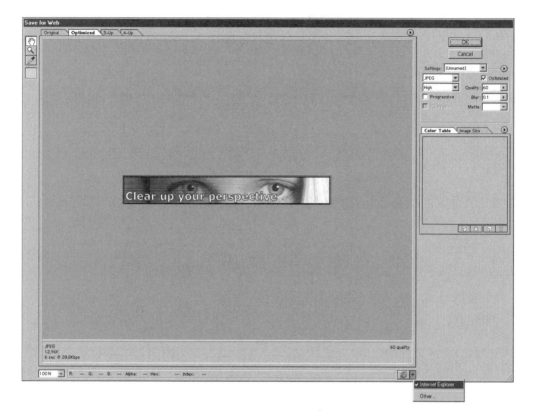

Seeing the Web Preview

After selecting the browser of your choice, the browser will appear with a copy of the Web graphic you're creating. This will give you a good idea of how the final image will appear in the Web browser.

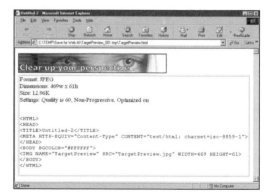

Importing Artwork

There will be times when you want to use bitmap images in your Illustrator artwork. You might, for example, want to use a photograph in a brochure. Images created in other programs, or scanned-in artwork, can be brought into your Illustrator documents.

Placing Photographs into Illustrator

There may be times when you'd like to add photographs, or some other type of bitmap image, to your Illustrator artwork. This is possible using two different methods. You can import bitmap images by linking to them or embedding them. To do so, choose File|Place.

Setting the Place Options

In the Place dialog box, browse to the file you wish to place into the current artwork and click Place to import the file into your artwork.

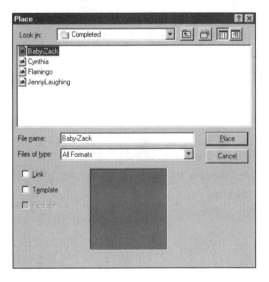

Linking Images

You can choose to link to the file you want to place into your artwork. This takes up less space when you save your Illustrator image and has the added benefit of using the most current version of the bitmapped file.

To link to the placed file, place a checkmark next to the Link option in the Place dialog box.

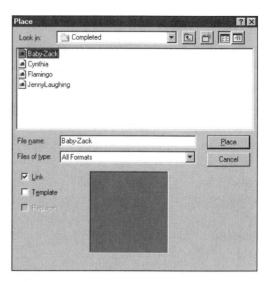

Templates

There may be times when you'd like to trace over a particular image. This is done using a template. The template is placed into the art-work as a dimmed image in a locked layer that can be traced over using Illustrator's various drawing tools.

Setting the Template Option

To place an image as a template, place a checkmark in the Place dialog box next to the Template option.

From Linked to Embedded Images

If you need to include the placed image with the artwork—to send it out to be printed, for example—you can do so.

To embed a currently linked file, choose Window|Show Links to open the Links palette.

Embedding Images

Click the small black arrow icon in the upper-right corner of the Links palette and choose Embed Image from the pull-down menu that appears.

Using Illustrator with Other Programs

Today, it's not uncommon to use several programs to accomplish any given task. You may, for example, use Illustrator to create buttons for a Web site, import the button images into Photoshop to add effects to them, and, finally, add the images to a Web page using GoLive. Not to worry, working with images from all these programs is a snap.

Illustrator and Photoshop

With Illustrator and Photoshop, you can actually just copy and paste artwork from Illustrator into Photoshop. Simply use the Selection tool to select an object, or group of objects, in Illustrator.

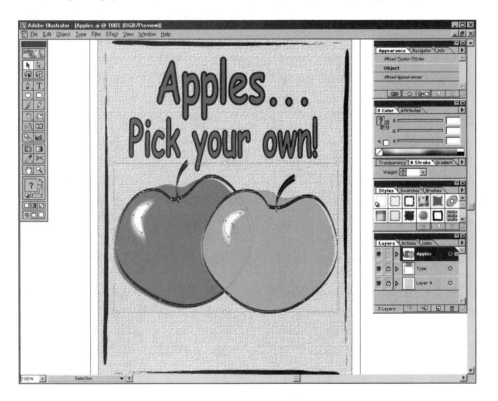

Copy in Illustrator

With the objects selected, choose Edit|Copy.

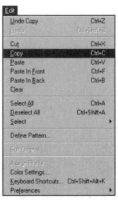

Paste into Photoshop

Open Photoshop, create a new image by choosing File|New, and then choose Edit|Paste to paste the objects created in Illustrator into the Photoshop image.

Illustrator and Acrobat

Artwork created in Illustrator can be exported to PDF without the need for Adobe Distiller. This makes it extremely easy to create final PDF documents. Simply create the artwork, including any text, in Illustrator, and, when you're done, choose File|Save As. Choose PDF from the File Type, as described earlier in this chapter, to save the artwork to a PDF file.

The PDF file can be opened in the Acrobat reader or in Acrobat itself by double-clicking its icon.

Opening a PDF Created in Illustrator

With the file opened in Acrobat you can make any changes necessary, including setting up password protection and other options.

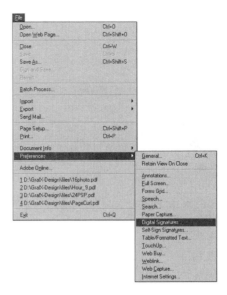

Illustrator and GoLive

Artwork created in Illustrator can be saved for the Web, as described earlier in the chapter. With the files saved as Web-ready artwork, they can be opened and used in GoLive.

To use any Illustrator artwork in GoLive, copy the files to the directory that's been set up for your Web images and open GoLive.

In GoLive, you can drag and drop files, and even drop them on the page icon to use them as background images.

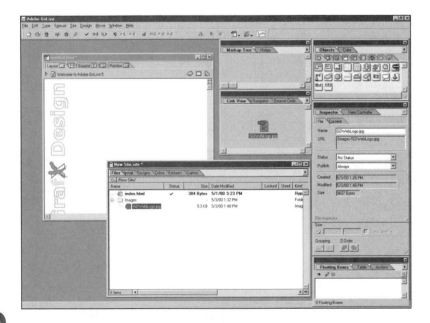

Chapter 3
Basic Drawing Techniques

- Draw shapes

- Group objects

- Draw lines

- Color your objects

- Fill shapes

- Use the brushes

- Use styles

- Change the order of objects

Drawing Shapes

Most artwork begins with the artist drawing some basic shapes. Illustrator has several tools and menu choices that enable you to easily draw and edit basic shapes.

Using the Shape Tools

The Shape tools are located in the Toolbox.

Two tools are shown in the Toolbox, and several others are available from the flyout. To access these other tools, click and hold your mouse over either tool. Doing so will open the flyout, allowing you to choose one of the other shapes.

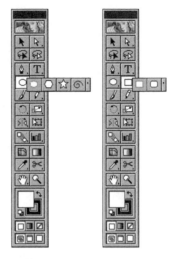

Adding Shapes

To add a shape to your illustration, select the shape you want and click and drag it onto the artboard.

By default, the shape will be drawn from the corner outwards. You can have the shape tool draw from the center outwards instead by holding down the Alt/Option key while dragging. You can also have the shapes keep an equal aspect ratio by holding down the Shift key while dragging.

Deleting Shapes

To delete a shape, you need to choose the shape first using the Selection tool. After activating the Selection tool, click on the shape you want to delete and press the Delete key. You can select several shapes at once by dragging the Selection tool over the shapes you want to select.

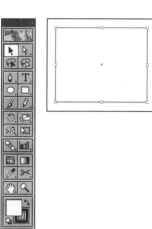

Moving Shapes

To move a shape, choose the shape with the Selection tool. With the shape selected, you can simply click and drag the shape anywhere in your drawing. The original shape will stay visible, and you'll also see an outline of the shape while it's being moved.

With the shape selected you can also nudge it using the cursor keys. This allows for very exact movement.

Copying Shapes

To copy a shape, choose the shape with the Selection tool and choose Edit|Copy from the menu. Optionally, you can hold down the Alt key on a PC or the Option key on a Macintosh when you drag a shape.

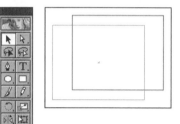

Pasting Shapes

To paste a copied shape elsewhere on your drawing, choose Edit|Paste from the menu. You can also paste objects directly in front of or behind the object you copied by choosing Paste In Front or Paste In Back, respectively.

Creating Object Groups

There will be times when you'll want to have several objects act as though they are actually one object. This can be achieved by grouping the objects together.

Grouping objects enables you to move them all together and apply strokes, fills, and styles to the objects all at once.

Grouping Objects

To group several objects, choose the objects with the Selection tool and choose Object|Group. The grouped objects will now behave much like one single object. Note that grouping objects may change the Fill and/or Stroke icons in the Toolbox. When objects with different fill/stroke values are selected, the Fill/Stroke icons may display a question mark. This just indicates that Illustrator can't show all of the different values.

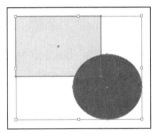

Ungrouping Objects

To ungroup objects, choose the group using the Selection tool and choose Object|Ungroup.

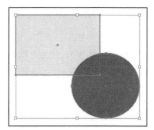

Drawing Lines

Being an illustration program, you'd expect Illustrator to enable you to draw all sorts of lines, and you'd be right. Several drawing tools with plenty of options enable you to draw all kinds of lines with Illustrator.

The Drawing Tools

Illustrator has three main drawing tools: the Pen tool, the Paintbrush tool, and the Pencil tool. Using these three tools, you can draw straight lines, smooth bezier curves, freehand brush, and freehand pencil lines.

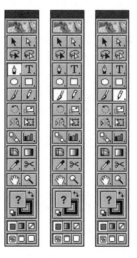

Drawing Straight Lines

To draw straight lines, select the Pen tool and click where you want the line to begin. Click once more where you want the line to end.

You can keep going by clicking on every point where you want a corner. You can draw triangles or even polygons in this manner. To end the polygon, click on the first point you created.

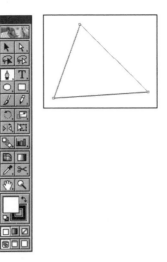

Drawing Smooth Curves

To draw smooth curves, select the Pen tool and click on the starting point. Move the pointer to where you want the other point on the curve to appear and click and drag the mouse to that point. You'll notice a control handle appear (it is a straight line running in two directions from the second point), and you'll be able to move the handle. Moving the handle will affect the curve, enabling you to draw smooth curves that would otherwise be impossible to draw freehand.

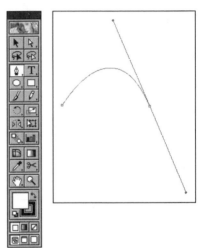

Using the Paintbrush Tool

The Paintbrush tool enables you to draw freehand brushstrokes. To use the Paintbrush tool, select it from the Toolbox and click and drag where you want the stroke to be drawn. Notice how the line's thickness varies depending on the direction of the stroke. You can change this, and apply different types of brushstrokes as well. We'll see how this is done later in the chapter.

Using the Pencil Tool

The Pencil tool is similar to the Paintbrush tool except that it draws lines with the same thickness throughout.

To draw freehand lines with the Pencil tool, select the Pencil tool from the Toolbox and click and drag where you want the line to be drawn.

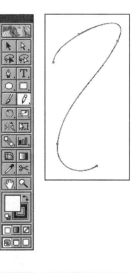

Smoothing Lines

Even though the lines drawn with the Pencil tool are quite smooth, you may want to smooth them even further. To do so, choose the line using the Selection tool, choose the Smooth tool from the flyout under the Pencil tool, and drag over the line where you want to smooth it.

You'll see a dotted line appear where you move the tool, which will dictate where the line will be smoothed.

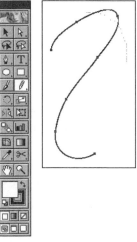

Setting the Stroke

Drawing programs generally refer to outlines, or lines, as strokes. You can change the size of the stroke you've drawn on any object. To do so, select the object or group of objects, and set the stroke size in the Stroke palette.

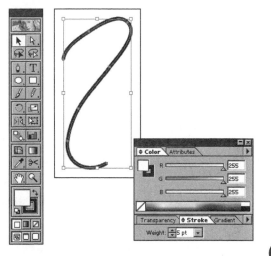

Coloring Your Objects

It wouldn't be very much fun drawing all of these shapes and lines if you couldn't color them or change their colors once you'd drawn them. No problem! Illustrator has several tools and methods you can use to add some color to your drawings.

The Color Swatches

Near the bottom of the Toolbox you'll find the color swatches. There's the Stroke, Fill, and Default Fill and Stroke icons.

You can click on either the Stroke or Fill icons to activate them. With either of them active, you can change the color of the stroke or fill of any selected object.

When you want to revert to the default white fill and black stroke, you can do so quickly by clicking on the Default Fill and Stroke icon (it's just below and to the left of the two color swatches).

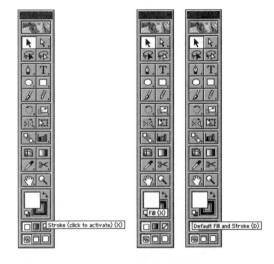

Setting a Color with the Color Palette

With either the Fill or Stroke icons selected, you can choose a new color by clicking and dragging the sliders in the Color palette. Note that which sliders are available will depend on the current color mode of the image you're working on.

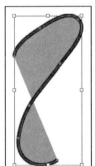

Choosing Colors from the Color Picker

Double-clicking on either the Fill or Stroke icon will bring up the Color Picker dialog box. You can choose a new color from within this dialog box by clicking in the main color swatch. You can further refine the color by moving the slider. If you know the value of the color you want, you can enter the numbers in decimal or hexadecimal. You can also restrict the choices to Web-safe colors only.

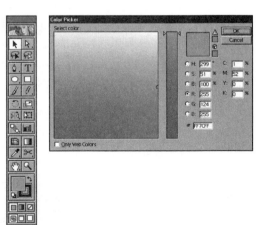

Setting the Fill Color of an Object

To set the fill color of an object, several objects, or a group, choose the object with the Selection tool, click on the Fill icon, and then set the color in the Color palette (or by double-clicking the Fill icon and choosing a new color from the Color Picker dialog box).

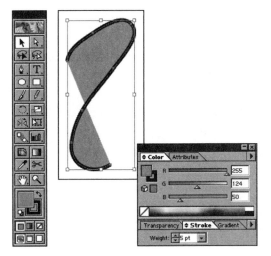

Setting the Stroke Color of an Object

Setting the stroke color of an object is as easy as setting the fill color. Simply select the object with the Selection tool, click on the Stroke icon, and set the color in the Color palette (or by double-clicking on the Stroke icon and choosing a new color from the Color Picker dialog box).

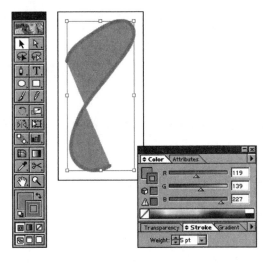

Setting the Stroke or Fill to None

What if you don't want an object to have any color? Easy. You can set either the stroke or fill to none (you can actually set both to none, but I've never found a good use for this).

You can do this by selecting the object, selecting either the fill or stroke by clicking on the Fill or Stroke icon, and then clicking on the None icon.

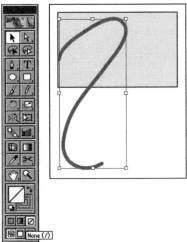

Using the Eyedropper Tool

You can set one object's fill and stroke colors based on another object's colors by using the Eyedropper tool. To do so, choose the object you wish to change using the Selection tool. With the object you want to change selected, click on the object whose properties you want to use with the Eyedropper tool.

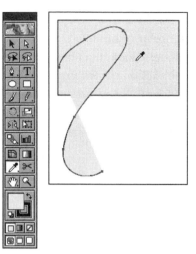

Filling Shapes

Aside from filling shapes and objects with color, you can also use gradients. These make it easy to get 3D effects and other effects, such as textures, using Illustrator.

Using Gradients

Gradients can be used to achieve metallic affects and add three-dimensionality to your images.

As with many of the things you can do in Illustrator, there are several ways to add a gradient to an object.

Adding a Gradient from the Stroke/Fill

You can quickly and easily add a gradient fill by clicking on the Fill icon and then clicking on the Gradient icon.

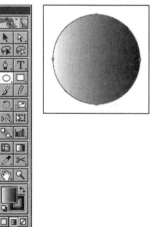

Using the Gradient Tool

You can also add a gradient to any selected object with the Gradient tool. To do so, choose the object with the Selection tool, select the Gradient tool, click where you want the gradient to start, drag to where you want the gradient to end, and release the mouse.

This method has the advantage of enabling you to position the start and end of the gradient as well as letting you set the angle of the gradient.

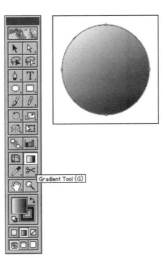

Accessing the Gradient Options

You can set the options of the Gradient tool via the Gradient palette. To access all of this tool's options, click on the small arrow icon in the upper-right corner of the Gradient palette and choose Show Options.

Setting the Gradient Tool Options

With the options visible, you can choose a type and set the angle or location. The location can be set for radial gradients, and the angle can be set for linear gradients.

You can also add and remove colors to create a custom gradient.

Adding Colors to a Gradient

To add a color to an existing gradient, simply click below the gradient bar. Doing so will add another slider.

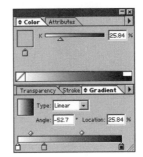

Resetting or Changing the Color Mode of a Gradient

Adding a slider may change the color mode of the gradient. To reset, or change, the color mode of the Gradient palette, click on the small arrow icon located in the upper right-hand corner of the Color palette and choose a color mode.

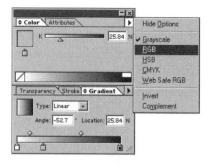

Changing the Colors in a Gradient

To change the color of a slider in the Gradient palette, click on the slider and then adjust the color in the Color palette. If an object is active and it contains the gradient fill, you'll notice that it updates in real-time as you make changes to the gradient.

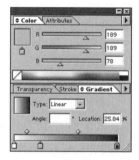

Removing Colors from a Gradient

To remove a color from the gradient, click and drag the slider off the palette. Doing so will remove the slider and its color from the gradient.

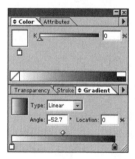

Moving Colors in a Gradient

You can move any of the colors in a gradient by simply clicking and dragging the slider. Doing so will change the appearance of the gradient.

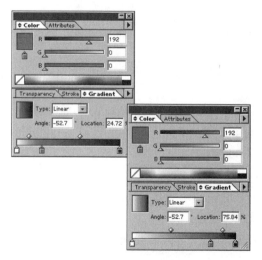

Changing the Way the Colors Interact

You can change the way that colors in a Gradient interact. To do so, move the diamond-shaped sliders at the top of the gradient bar. You can compress and expand the colors to change the appearance of the gradient.

Using the Brushes

Illustrator includes a number of preset brushes—everything from calligraphic brushes to patterns and arrows. You can apply the different brushes to lines and shapes.

Accessing the Brushes

To access the various types of brushes available, click on the small arrow icon in the upper right-hand corner of the Brushes palette. You can choose which types of brushes should show up in the palette.

By default, all of the brush types are available.

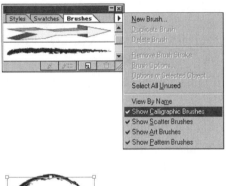

Using a Brush

To use a brush on a line or shape, choose the line or shape with the Selection tool and then click on the brush you want to apply to the object.

Removing a Brush Stroke

To remove a brush stroke and return the stroke of an object to its default, select the object with the Selection tool and click on the arrow icon in the Brush palette. From the menu, choose Remove Brush Stroke.

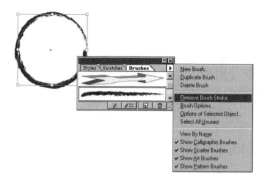

Using Styles

Objects can have styles applied to them in Illustrator. A style stays with an object until it is removed, in much the same manner as brush strokes. Although styles may seem more involved than brush strokes, they are just as easy to apply.

You can apply styles such as drop shadows to objects, and these styles will remain in effect through any size or other changes.

Applying Styles

Applying styles is as easy as selecting the object you wish to apply the style to and selecting the style from the Styles palette.

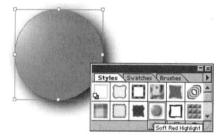

Setting the Style Palette Options

To set the Style palette options, click the arrow icon in the upper-right corner of the Styles palette and choose the Palette option.

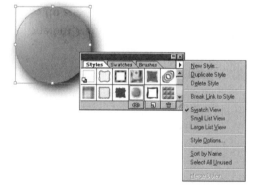

Removing a Style from an Object

To remove a style from an object, select the object with the Selection tool and choose the Default style from the Style Options menu.

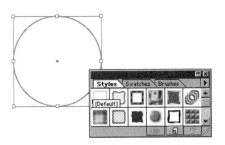

Changing the Order of Objects

Because Illustrator is object oriented, all of the objects you draw (shapes, lines, etc.) can be moved about easily in the XY plane. Because of the object-oriented nature of the objects you draw, you can also place objects in front of and behind other objects. In essence, you can change the stacking order of any object you create or import into Illustrator.

Moving Objects to the Front

To move an object forward, or to the front, select the object with the Selection tool and choose Object|Arrange|Bring To Front or Object| Arrange|Bring Forward.

Moving an object forward will move it one place forward (towards the top of the stack, if you will), while moving an object to the front will bring it to the top of the stack, above all other objects.

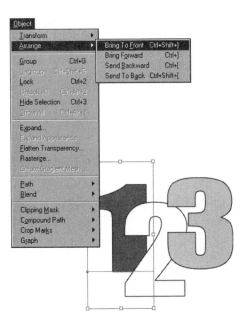

Moving Objects to the Back

To move an object backward, or to the back, select the object with the Selection tool and choose Object|Arrange|Send To Back or Object|Arrange|Send Backward.

Moving an object backward will move it one place backwards (towards the bottom of the stack, if you will), while moving an object to the back will send it to the bottom of the stack, below all other objects. Remember that you can also Cut an object and then Paste it in front of or behind another object using the Paste In Front or Paste In Back command.

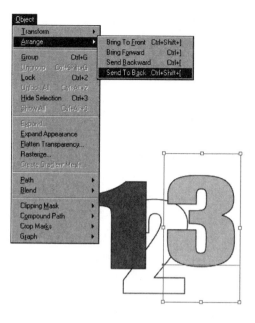

Chapter 4
Anchor Point
Editing Techniques

- Add points

- Delete points

- Convert points

- Move points

Working with Illustrator Editing Techniques

Illustrations created with Illustrator consist of paths—one or more straight or curved segments—and you have a great deal of control over the shape of those curved paths and segments. They begin and end with anchor points; by editing the anchor points, you can change the shape of the segments and paths. You can change the shape of a curve by dragging the direction points at the end of direction lines that appear at anchor points. This chapter shows how this is done.

Anchor Points

Anchor points—recognized as small circles—are visible at the ends of segments and paths. The circles will be outlined when the point is not selected, and they will be filled when a point is selected. Before you can manipulate an anchor point, you must first select it. You can choose all points with the Selection tool or individual points with the Direct Selection tool and Group Selection tool.

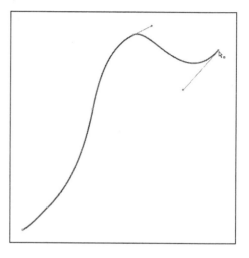

Segments

Segments are curves that exist between points. You can manipulate segments, as well as points, by clicking and dragging them with the Direct Selection tool. As you drag the segment, you can see the effect that the change will have in real-time. To complete the change, simply release the mouse button.

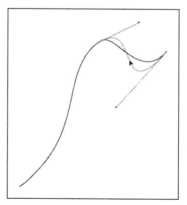

Direction Points

Direction points and direction handles enable you to fine-tune curves. You can click and drag a direction point using the Direct Selection tool. As you drag, you will see the effect the change has on the curve. Once you have the curve bent into the shape you want, release the mouse button to complete the change.

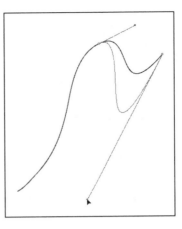

Smooth Points

There are two types of points: smooth points and corner points. Smooth points have smooth continuous curves associated with them.

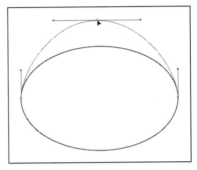

Corner Points

Corner points, the second type of point, have abrupt path changes associated with them. Paths change directions sharply at corner points.

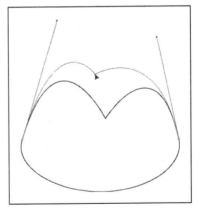

Selecting Points and Segments

Before you can manipulate a point, a group of points, or a segment, you must select it using one of Illustrator's several selection tools. These tools are grouped at the top of the Tool palette. Clockwise from the upper left are the Selection tool, the Direct Selection tool and the Group Selection tool, the Lasso tool, and the Direct Select Lasso tool.

The Direct Selection tool and the Group Selection tool share a spot on the Tool palette. To toggle from one to the other, click and hold the mouse over the tool to access the flyout menu.

Selection Tool

The Selection tool doesn't select points or segments. Rather, it selects all of the points and segments associated with an object. When you've done so, the object will have a bounding box around it. Any changes, such as moving a point or segment, will also affect the rest of the points and segments associated with the selected object.

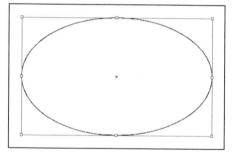

Direct Selection Tool

The Direct Selection tool enables you to select a segment or point directly. Once selected, a point or segment will display its direction points and lines. You can then click and drag the direction points to manipulate the point or segment separately from the rest of the object.

To select a point with the Direct Selection tool, click and drag around the point you want to select. You can also select a path or segment by clicking and dragging around it.

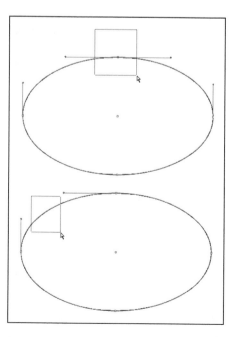

Group Selection Tool

With objects grouped, the Selection tool will select all of them. The Group Selection tool, on the other hand, enables you to select an object from within a group of objects. It also enables you to select a group from within multiple groups in the artwork. Each additional click adds objects or groups to the selection.

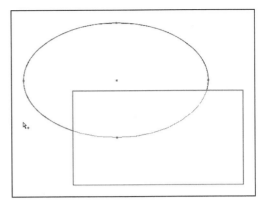

Lasso Tool

Using the Lasso tool, you can select all of the points and segments on an object separately from other objects. To do so, simply click and drag around any visible portion of the object.

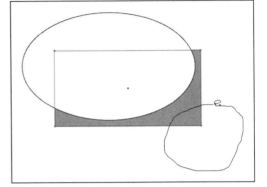

Direct Select Lasso Tool

The Direct Select Lasso tool enables you to select points and segments by clicking and dragging around them. The Direct Select Lasso tool, like the Lasso tool, is a freeform tool, so you can drag in any manner that's needed to select the segments or points you want to choose.

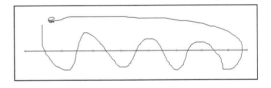

Adding Anchor Points

By adding points to a path or shape and by manipulating the different points, you can actually create very sophisticated objects. To add points to a segment, select the Add Anchor Point tool (it's available under the Pen tool flyout) and click anywhere on a segment.

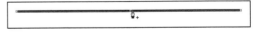

Deleting Anchor Points

You can delete points from a path or segment using the Delete Anchor Point tool, which is available under the Pen tool flyout. To delete an existing point, select the Delete Anchor Point tool and click on the point to be deleted.

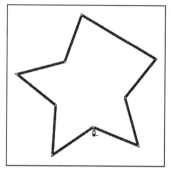

Splitting Paths

You can split a path using the Scissors tool. To do this, select the Scissors tool and click on the segment you want to split. The split will not be immediately evident, but you can select the point where the path was cut, using the Direct Selection tool, and move the two ends apart.

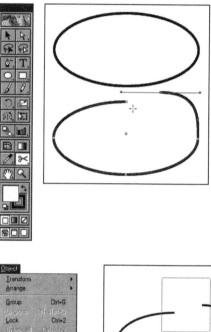

Joining Points

You can close open paths by selecting the end points, using the Direct Selection tool, and then joining them. To do this, select the endpoints of the path and choose Object|Path|Join. The points you selected will be joined, a straight line will now exist between the ends, and the path will be closed.

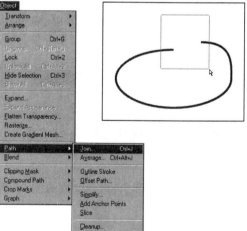

Slicing Paths

Using the Knife tool, you can slice a path into many broken segments. To do so, select the Knife tool and draw it over the path where you want the path to be sliced.

Slicing an object creates many new objects that can be moved and manipulated separately.

Converting Anchor Points

You can convert from one type of anchor point to another, and back again. To convert an anchor point, select the Convert Anchor Point tool and click on the point to be converted.

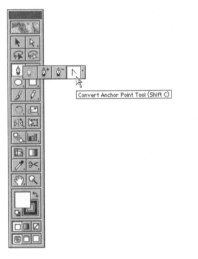

Converting Smooth Points to Corner Points

To convert a smooth point into a corner point, simply click on the point to be converted with the Convert Anchor Point tool. You'll note that the formerly smooth point now has a distinct point.

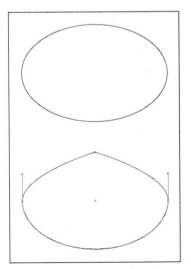

Converting Smooth Points to Corner Points with Independent Direction Lines

You can also convert a smooth point to a corner point with independent direction lines. To do so, select the Convert Anchor Point tool and click and drag on one of the direction points.

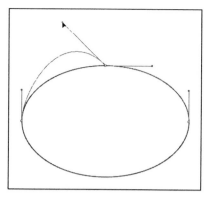

Converting Corner Points to Smooth Points

You can convert a corner point to a smooth point by selecting the Convert Anchor Point tool and clicking and dragging on a corner point. Doing so will cause the direction lines to appear and will enable you to smooth out the curve.

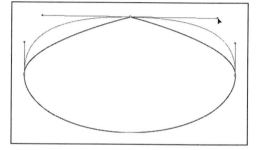

Direction Points

Direction points are situated at the ends of direction lines. Dragging direction points allows you to smooth and shape curves and corners. If the direction points are not visible, click on the anchor point you want to change with the Direct Selection tool. This will activate the direction lines and points. Click and drag the direction point to shape the curve, or the corner, into a new shape. You can actually create fairly complex shapes from other simple shapes, such as making a heart from an ellipse.

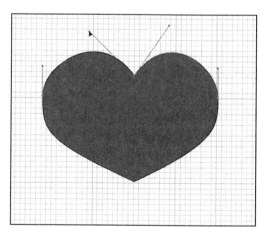

You may want to turn on the grid (View|Show Grid) to help adjust the placement of direction points, as shown in several figures.

Moving Anchor Points

You can move anchor points around to create new shapes. To move points, you need to select them first, which you can do using the Direct Selection tool.

Moving Separate Anchor Points

You can move a separate anchor point by click-ing and dragging it with the Direct Selection tool. Additionally, you can move the point by using the cursor keys once the point is selected. To make larger movements, hold the Shift key while pressing the cursor keys.

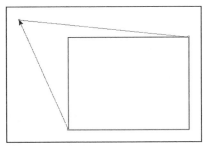

Moving Groups of Anchor Points

To move a group of points in unison, select the points you want to move. You can do so on a PC by Ctrl-clicking the points, or by Shift-click-ing on a Mac, or by using the Direct Select Lasso tool. With the points selected, simply click and drag them into place using the Direct Selection tool. You can also use the cursor keys to move them once you have selected the points.

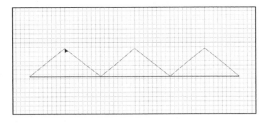

Restricting the Angle of Movement

You can restrict the angle of movement when you move a point, or points, by holding down the Shift key as you move the points. The angle used can be set under Edit|Preferences|General. You can also set the amount that cursor keys will move objects and anchor points with the same dialog box.

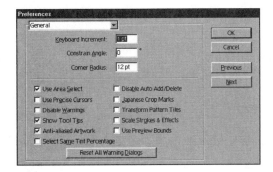

Redrawing Lines with the Pencil Tool and Brush Tool

After drawing a line, you may not be satisfied with it. You can choose Edit|Undo, of course, but you can also redraw the line. To do so, move the Brush tool or the Pencil tool near where you want to make the correction, and simply redraw the line. If the line has been deselected, select the line again using the Direct Selection tool before redrawing it.

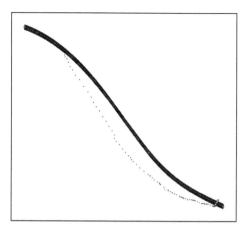

As you redraw the line, you'll see a faint broken line in blue. This represents where the new line will be drawn.

Using the Smooth Tool

Sometimes you might find that lines are not as smooth as you would like. To smooth out a previously drawn line, or to smooth out the segments drawn between anchor points, select the Smooth tool (under the Pencil tool flyout) and drag the tool over the line you want smoothed.

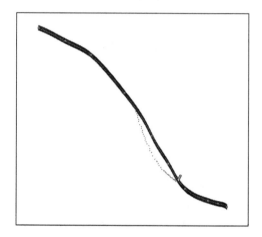

As you drag the tool over the line, you'll see a broken blue line being drawn. This line indicates how the smoothing will affect the line. The new line may have fewer points than the original line.

Setting the Smooth Tool Options

You can set the options for the Smooth tool by double-clicking on its icon in the Tool palette. This will bring up the Smooth Tool Preferences dialog box. You can set the Tolerances to control the smoothness and complexity of lines. Higher numbers yield smoother lines. You can also set the Smoothness percentage. This setting controls how smooth lines are drawn; higher numbers yield smoother curves.

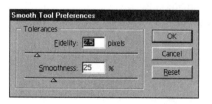

Chapter 5
Layer Basics

- Use layers

- Use the Layers palette

- Add layers

- Delete layers

- Move layers

The Power of Layers

Using layers is a very powerful way to help you organize your image objects. You can create, reorder, and delete layers, and you can split objects into separate layers. If I had to choose what I thought was the most powerful tool a digital graphic program offers to an artist, I would choose layers. This chapter shows you how to use them.

What Layers Are

Think of layers as being sheets of acetate. If you drew something on a sheet of acetate and then added a new sheet on top of the first, you would still be able to see the object(s) on the first layer. If you drew an object on the new layer, it might, or might not, obscure the objects on the layers below. This is similar to how layers work in Illustrator. There's much more you can do with digital layers, though, as you'll soon discover.

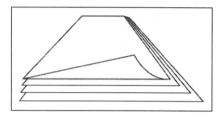

Why You Should Use Layers

Layers help you organize your work. You can move layers—in other words, change their order—so that they can be moved up or down in the stack. You can also change the transparency of objects in a layer, so as to allow objects in underlying layers to show through at different rates.

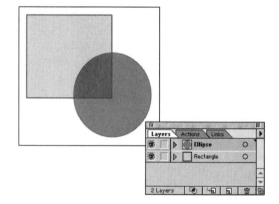

Anatomy of the Layers Palette

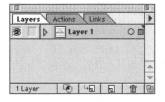

The Layers palette (choose Window|Show Layers) is fairly simple to work with. It's grouped together with the Actions and Links palettes by default.

Below the Layer tab, you'll see the current layers associated with your image. A layer may have the following icons associated with it: a visibility icon (which resembles an eye), a lock icon, a small arrow icon (which expands and collapses the layer and sublayers), the layer name, the Appearance icon (a small circle), a small icon that will be visible when any objects on the current layer are selected, and a small black triangle that, if visible, indicates the layer is active.

Along the bottom of the Layers palette you'll find several more icons: Make/Release Clipping Mask, Create New Sublayer, Create New Layer, and Delete Selection.

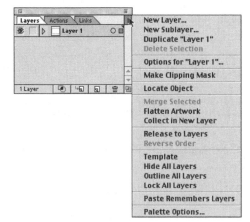

You'll also see a small black arrow in the upper-right corner of the Layers palette. Clicking on this activates the Layers palette menu from which you can choose different options that affect how the layers in your image interact. We'll make use of many of these selections during the course of this book.

Changing the Visibility of a Layer

The visibility icon is a toggle. If the layer is currently visible, clicking on it will turn off the layer's visibility. If the layer is not currently visible, clicking on it will turn on the layer.

Locking a Layer

Locking a layer prevents objects on that layer from being selected or edited. You can toggle a layer's lock status by clicking on the Lock icon.

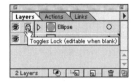

Naming a Layer

You can change the name of any layer to better organize your work. To do so, double-click on the layer name in the Layers palette to bring up the Layer Options dialog box. In addition to changing the name in this dialog box, you can change the layer to a Template, lock the layer, set its visibility, set whether it will print or not, determine whether you can preview it or not, and set the dimming percentage. You can also set the layer's color.

Setting a Layer's Appearance

You can apply appearance attributes to a layer. To do so, click on the target icon. This cycles through three stages. When the icon resembles a small hollow circle, the layer is not targeted. When the icon resembles two circles, the layer is targeted but has no appearance attributes applied to it. When the icon resembles a small 3D sphere, the layer is targeted and has appearance attributes associated with it.

Converting a Layer to a Clipping Mask

As you'll see in Chapter 6, you can use the objects on one layer as a clipping mask for objects on another layer. To convert a layer to a clipping mask, simply click on the Make/ Release Clipping Mask icon.

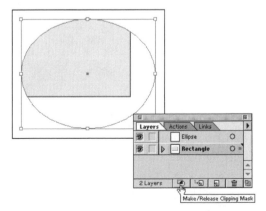

Adding New Sublayers

Sublayers help you organize the objects on a layer. In fact, creating a new object on a layer automatically creates a new sublayer. You can also create a new sublayer by clicking on the Create New Sublayer icon.

Sublayers share some of the same properties of layers. You can name them and target them for appearance attributes. You can also change their order. To view the sublayers of any given layer, simply click on the small arrow icon to the left of the layer name.

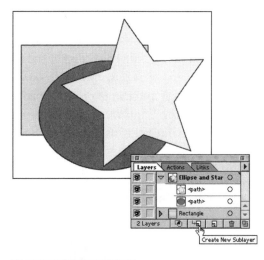

Adding New Layers

You can add new layers by clicking on the Create New Layer icon. New layers come in above the current layer.

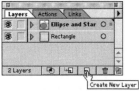

Deleting Layers

You can delete, or remove, layers from your image by making the layer current and clicking on the Delete Selection icon. You can also drag and drop a layer onto the trash icon to remove the layer.

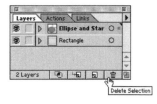

Changing the Order of Layers

You can reorder layers and sublayers by clicking and dragging them. For example, to move one layer above another existing layer, click and drag the layer into its new position.

Accessing the Layer Menu

All of the layer options we've seen so far, as well as a few others, can be accessed from the Layer menu. To access this, click on the small black arrow icon in the upper-right corner of the Layers palette. You will see the different choices you can access in the pull-down menu that appears.

Some of the options that are not available through the palette icons are described in the following sections.

Duplicating a Layer

You can duplicate a layer with all of its sublayers and objects by selecting the layer you want duplicated and choosing Duplicate "*Layer name*" from the Layers palette pull-down menu. Note that all current layers will be displayed in the pull-down menu.

Exploring Layer Options

You can see, and change, the options for a layer by choosing Options for "*Layer name*" from the Layers palette pull-down menu. The "Options" option will appear only for the currently active layer.

Locating Objects

You can locate an object in the Layers palette by selecting the object in your artwork and then choosing Locate Object in the Layers palette pull-down menu. The Layers palette will scroll and, if necessary, expand layer entries to show you where the object is located within the layer hierarchy.

Merging Selected Layers

You can merge selected layers together into a single layer. To do so, you must first select the layers. You can choose contiguous layers by Shift-clicking them, or choose multiple non-contiguous layers by Ctrl-clicking on a PC or Command-clicking on a Mac. Once the layers you want to merge are selected, choose Merge Selected from the Layers palette pull-down menu.

Flattening Your Artwork

You can merge all layers, selected or not, into a single layer by flattening your artwork. To do so, choose Flatten Artwork from the Layers palette pull-down menu. Note that all of the objects will still occupy separate sublayers.

Collecting Selected Objects in a New Layer

You can collect selected objects into a new layer. Note that this leaves the objects intact on their current layers. They are not copied, but the original layers become sublayers of the new layer.

To collect the objects into a new layer, select the objects and choose Collect in New Layer from the Layer palette pull-down menu.

Releasing Objects to New Layers

If you have a collection of objects on a layer, you can release the objects into separate layers. To do so, activate the layer with the objects you want released by clicking on the layer's name in the Layers palette and choosing Release to Layers from the Layers palette pull-down menu.

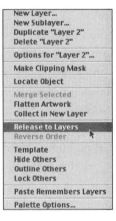

Reversing the Order of Layers

You can reverse the order of selected layers by selecting the layers being reversed (by Shift-clicking them) and choosing Reverse Order from the Layers palette pull-down menu. You can also reverse the order of noncontiguous layers by selecting them using Ctrl-click on a PC or Command-click on a Mac.

Hiding Layers

You can turn the visibility of a layer on and off by clicking on the second icon from the left in the layer's entry in the Layers palette. It can be quite tedious, however, if you have a number of layers you want to hide. Fortunately, you can turn off the visibility of all non-current layers by choosing Hide Others from the Layers palette pull-down menu.

Showing All Layers

You can also turn on the visibility of all layers in your artwork by choosing Show All Layers from the Layers palette pull-down menu.

Outlining Layers

You can put all but the current layer into out-line mode. This can make screen redraws much faster on a slower system. It also has the effect of keeping all objects visible while making them less intrusive when you work on your artwork.

To set the mode of all objects not on the current layer to outline mode, choose Outline Others from the Layers palette pull-down menu.

Previewing Layers

You can set the mode of all non-current layers back to preview mode by choosing Preview All Layers from the Layers palette pull-down menu. This will make all of the objects in your artwork visible in preview mode.

Locking Layers

You can lock layers individually by clicking on the lock icon next to the layer you want locked. There may be times, however, when you want to lock all layers but the one you're currently working on. To do so, choose Lock Others from the Layers palette pull-down menu.

Unlocking Layers

Just as you might want to lock a large number of layers, you might also want to unlock all locked layers in your artwork. To do so, simply choose Unlock All Layers from the Layers palette pull-down menu.

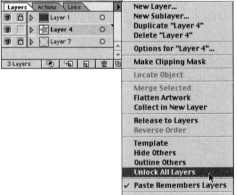

Pasting and Remembering

You can move an object from one layer to another by cutting and pasting it. To be sure that the object gets pasted into the layer you've chosen, make sure that Paste Remembers Layers is *not* selected.

After cutting the object, you can select a layer where you want the object pasted and choose either Paste, Paste In Front, or Paste In Back. Pasting places the object in the middle of the artwork, pasting in front places the object in its old location but above all other objects in the current layer, and pasting in back does the same but places the object behind all others in the current layer.

Note that copying and pasting to a new layer will not work if you choose Paste In Front or Paste In Back.

Palette Options

You can set certain Layers palette options by choosing Palette Options from the Layers palette pull-down menu. This brings up the Layers Palette Options dialog box.

Show Layers Only

Selecting Show Layers Only shows you only the layers in the Layers palette and does not allow you access to the sublayers.

Small Row Size

You can choose to view the layers in a small format by choosing Small for the row size in the Layers Palette Options dialog box.

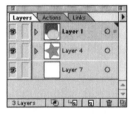

Medium Row Size

You can choose to view the layers in a medium format (the default) by choosing Medium for the row size in the Layers Palette Options dialog box.

Large Row Size

You can choose to view the layers in a large format by choosing Large for the row size in the Layers Palette Options dialog box. This is a good choice if you run Illustrator on a high-resolution screen where the icons in the Layers palette may be too small to be seen easily.

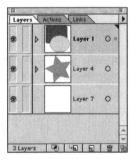

Custom Row Size

You even have the option of setting your own size for the layers in the Layers palette. To set a custom size, choose Palette Options from the Layers palette pull-down menu, select Other for the row size, and enter a value, in pixels, for the size you want.

Thumbnails

You can customize your Layers palette further by deciding which icons, or thumbnails, will be visible.

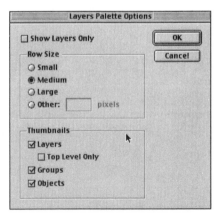

Layer Thumbnails

To toggle the Layers thumbnails on and off, choose Palette Options from the Layers palette pull-down menu and place or remove the checkmark in the Layers option under the Thumbnails Settings.

Group Thumbnails

To toggle the Group thumbnails on and off, choose Palette Options from the Layers palette pull-down menu and place or remove the checkmark in the Group option under the Thumbnails Settings.

Objects Thumbnails

To toggle the Objects thumbnails on and off, choose Palette Options from the Layers palette pull-down menu and place or remove the checkmark in the Objects option under the Thumbnails Settings.

Chapter 6
Masking Techniques

- Use masks

- Create clipping masks

- Create complex masks

- Add strokes and fills to masks

- Create opacity masks

The Power of Masks

Masks are powerful tools that can help you create effects that might otherwise be impossible. As mysterious and powerful as masks may seem to the uninitiated, they are relatively easy to understand and use. Several types of masks are available to you in Illustrator, and this chapter discusses them all.

Masks are used to mask off an area of one or several objects using another object. This may sound a little confusing, so I'll show you what I mean.

Creating Your First Mask

To create your first mask, follow along with the next several steps. I'll show you how to take two shapes and mask one of them with the other to create a new shape. To get started, I'll draw a couple of shapes that can be used to create a new shape using a mask.

Creating a Circle

Using the Ellipse tool, draw a circle.

To get a perfect circle with the Ellipse tool, hold down the Shift key while dragging with the mouse. (The figures in this section show shapes with colored fills, because at this point you should be able to fill shapes. You don't have to color your shapes if you don't want to, however.)

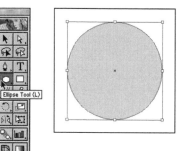

Creating a Star Shape

Click and hold the mouse over the Ellipse Tool until the flyout menu appears, and then select the Star tool. While placing the mouse somewhere around the upper-right side of the circle you just drew, click and drag the mouse upward and to the right to draw a star over the upper right side of the circle.

If the star isn't placed quite as you want it, drag it into place using the Selection tool.

Selecting Both Shapes

Using the Selection Tool, drag a marquee around both shapes to select them. You must have both shapes selected to create a mask. The top shape works as a mask on the underlying shape(s).

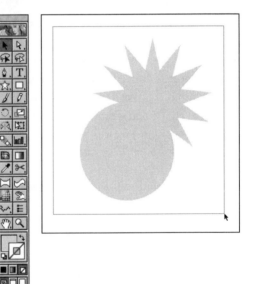

Creating the Mask

Click on the Make/Release Clipping Mask icon on the Layers palette. This will create a new clipping mask using the two selected shapes.

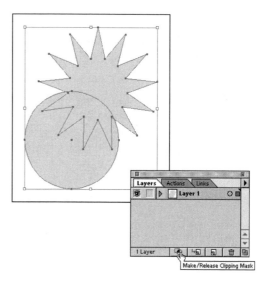

Seeing the Results

You should see a new shape created from the two original shapes. The new shape is the result of the upper shape "masking" the lower shape. Because only two shapes are used in our example, it doesn't really matter which is the upper shape and which is the lower shape. The outcome will result in a similar shape, regardless.

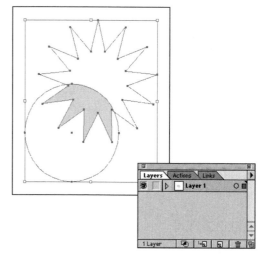

Viewing the Mask

You can see the mask you've created by selecting it. To do so, choose Edit|Select|Masks. This will reveal, in this case at least, that the star shape is being used as the mask over the circle—the lower shape.

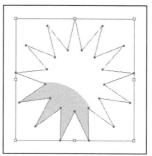

Modifying the Mask

With the mask selected, you can modify it as you would any other shape. You could, for example, move it or stretch it. This will reveal more or less of the underlying object. (The tools for modifying a shape are discussed elsewhere in this book.)

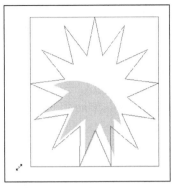

Locking the Mask

To prevent the mask from being modified, you can lock it. To lock a mask, select it using Edit| Select|Masks and then choose Object|Lock.

Grouping the Object and the Mask

You can group the object and its mask together. When you group an object with its mask, they will move together as one object. If you don't group an object with its mask, you can move either one, thereby changing the appearance of the object created from the original objects.

To group an object with its mask, simply select both the object and the mask and choose Object|Group. You can, of course, ungroup an object at a later time by selecting it and choosing Object|Ungroup.

Releasing the Mask

If you decide that you no longer need the mask you've created, you can release the mask. To release a mask, activate the layer containing the mask, and the masked object, by clicking on its name in the Layers palette, and then click on the Make/Release Clipping Mask icon.

Back to the Original Images

Releasing a mask gives you back the various original objects. All, that is, except for the object that resulted from the mask. This object is still there, but it has been changed. You won't actually see the mask because both its stroke and fill values have been set to None.

To see the object that resulted from the mask, select the object (you can do so by selecting the visible object and then choosing Edit| Select|Inverse) and then change either its stroke or fill.

Creating a More Complex Mask

Now that you've seen how easy it is to create a mask, it's time to learn something a little more complex.

This section shows you how to use type and a bitmap image to create the effect of type filled with a photographic image. You will need a scanned photograph to follow along with the steps that follow.

Placing the Photograph

The effect I want is that of a photograph seemingly placed into some type. To start the artwork, you'll need to place a photographic image into Illustrator. To do so, choose File|Place, browse to the image you want to use, and click on Place.

Adding Some Type

Select the Type tool and enter some text over the photograph. You can do as I have done and create a new layer for the text, which will keep things a little tidier.

Resizing the Type

You'll need to resize the text so that it covers the photograph. Choose the Selection tool and click on the text. With the text selected, click and drag the corners of the bounding box to stretch the type over the entire photograph.

Positioning the Type

If necessary, you can move the type into position over the photograph. To do so, choose the Selection tool and click and drag the text into place.

Creating the Mask

It's time to create the mask. Choose both the photograph and the text using the Selection tool. With both objects selected, click on the Make/Release Clipping Mask icon in the Layers palette.

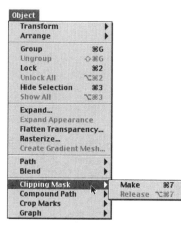

Examining the Masked Object

You should end up with something that resembles text filled with a photograph. If necessary, you can move the mask or the object around to better place the photograph within the text.

Adding a Stroke

The artwork looks pretty good, but a nice dark stroke around the text would help it stand out and add a touch of professionalism. To add a stroke, select the photograph and the mask and click on the Default Fill and Stroke icon in the Toolbox (or just press the "D" key).

You can now widen the stroke by setting a higher value in the Stroke palette.

The Finished Artwork

Your final artwork should show stroked text filled with a photograph.

Creating Opacity Masks

I mentioned that a couple of types of masks are available in Illustrator. I've just demonstrated some examples of using clipping masks, and now I'll show you how to create and use an opacity mask. Opacity masks enable you to change the opacity of the mask, thereby letting more or less of the underlying object(s) show through.

You can easily use gradients as a means of applying a variable mask to underlying objects. To see how this works, follow along with the next example.

Creating Some Text

Using the Type Tool, enter some text. I entered a couple of numbers spaced out, adding an extra space between each character.

Locking the Text

Lock the text so that it won't accidentally be selected when you select the mask and the masked object later. You can lock the text by clicking on the Lock icon next to the layer name in the Layers palette.

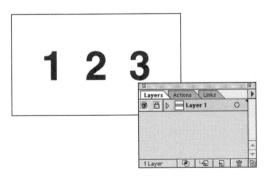

Creating a Rectangle

Create a new layer and add a rectangle. This rectangle should completely cover the text. (I chose to color the shapes in this section; you don't have to do this if you don't want to, however.)

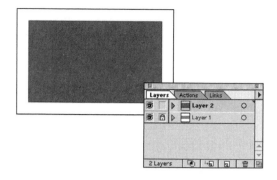

Creating an Ellipse

Create another new layer and, using the Ellipse tool, add an ellipse centered over the rectangle. This ellipse will become the new opacity mask.

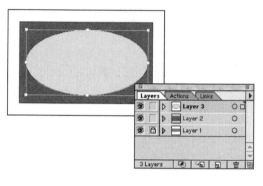

Setting the Stroke to None

Set the Stroke to None, because you don't want the stroke to have any bearing on the mask. All you want is a gradient opacity mask with no stroke.

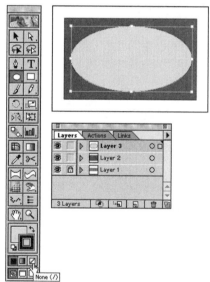

Setting the Fill to Gradient

Set the fill to Gradient by clicking on the Gradient icon below the Fill and Stroke icons in the Toolbox. You need to set the fill to a gradient to see the effects of having an opacity mask.

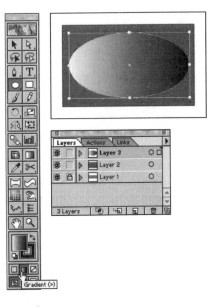

Adding a New Gradient

If necessary, select the Gradient tool and change the gradient fill on the ellipse. You want a gradient that goes from white on the left to black on the right. Later you can play with the gradient settings to experiment with how this will affect the underlying objects. For now, just follow along so you'll have a good idea of how the opacity mask works.

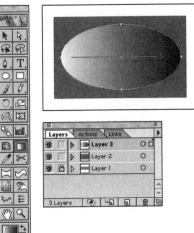

Selecting the Rectangle and the Ellipse

You'll be creating the opacity mask from the ellipse and using it to affect the opacity of the underlying rectangle. To do so, choose both the rectangle and the ellipse using the Selection tool.

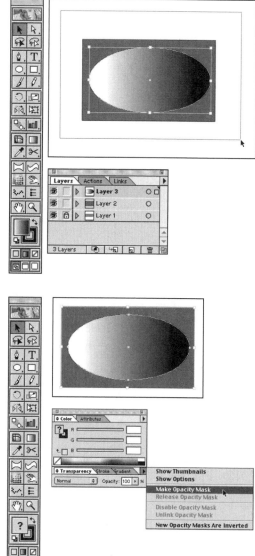

Creating the Opacity Mask

It's time to create the opacity mask. You will find the menu control in the Transparency palette. Click on the Transparency tab to bring up the Transparency palette, or choose Window|Show Transparency.

Click on the small black arrow icon to the right of the palette and choose Make Opacity Mask.

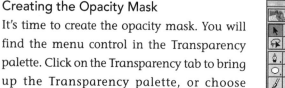

The Final Masked Image

You should end up with a rectangle with a fading ellipse that allows the underlying numbers to show through. The numbers show through most where the mask was black and least where the mask was white. This is because the white area masks more of the underlying object than the black area does. In my example, the number "1" does not show through at all because the mask hides it.

Chapter 7
Filters and Effects

- Change color modes

- Combine shapes

- Distort and transform objects

- Work with vectors and bitmaps

- Stylize your objects

- Apply bitmap effects

Using Filters and Effects

Sometimes a simple object or collection of objects is just not enough. (In Illustrator, every path or shape is called an object.) You'll find there are times when you need to combine objects in different ways or manipulate them to achieve the effect you're after. That's where filters and effects come in.

In this chapter, you'll learn how to distort your objects, how to combine them in new ways, and how to apply different filters and effects to them.

Colors

Colors are as important in digital art as in any other media. It is much easier, however, to change colors with digital art.

Illustrator provides a couple of color modes to work with. The color mode you choose will generally be defined, at least in part, by the intended use of the final image.

For example, if the final image is intended for the Web, you should stick with Web-safe colors. If the image you're creating is intended for print, you should use CMYK (Cyan, Magenta, Yellow, and a percentage of blacK), which refers to the colors of inks used by printing presses. If you're using the image with onscreen uses in mind, you should use RGB (Red, Green, and Blue), which refers to the gamut of colors you see on a computer screen.

Choosing Color Modes

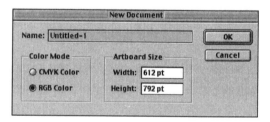

When you open a new image in Illustrator, you're presented with a dialog box asking you to choose the color mode. You should choose the mode with the final destination of the image in mind.

Changing Color Modes

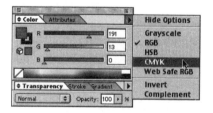

If you've selected one color mode and later decide that the image should use another mode, don't worry because you can easily change modes. To change your artwork's color mode, click on the small, black, arrow icon in the upper-right corner of the Color palette and choose from one of the selections in the menu.

You should be aware that some color modes have a smaller number of colors available. When switching to a more limited palette, you may lose some of the integrity of your artwork.

The Different Color Modes

Again, several color modes are available in Illustrator. To see which mode you're currently using, simply take a look at the Color palette. You'll see the swatches and sliders for each color labeled with the letters that represent their place in the name of the color mode.

Note that, unless you select all objects in an image, the Color mode change will affect only currently selected objects or new objects created with the different color mode.

Grayscale

Grayscale uses white, black, and 256 grays. You may want to choose this mode if you are printing in black and white only.

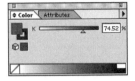

RGB

As mentioned earlier, RGB is the color mode to choose if the images you are creating are intended for on-screen use. Each of the red, green, and blue tones can have values from 0 to 255 (for a total of 256 values). When each is set to 0, the color is black; when each is set to 255, the result is white.

Using RGB mode, it is possible to create approximately 16.7 million colors.

HSB

HSB, which stands for Hue, Saturation, and Brightness, is essentially the same color mode as RGB and uses exactly the same number of colors. The difference lies in how these colors are described. RGB uses decimal values from 1 to 255 for each of the red, green, and blue tones, whereas HSB uses degrees and percentages: between 0° and 360° of the Hue (color); a percentage from 0% (gray) to 100% (fully saturated) for Saturation (strength or purity of color); and a percentage from 0% (black) to 100% (white) for Brightness. Some artists find this a more natural way to use color.

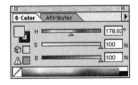

CMYK

CMYK refers to the colors of the inks used in printing. K refers to black (because B is already used for blue). Black ink is needed because, due to imperfections in the inks used, it would be impossible to get pure black by mixing the inks. CMYK has fewer colors available than RGB.

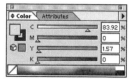

Web-Safe RGB

Web-safe RGB is a small subset of colors used for what is commonly referred to as the Web-safe palette. This palette contains 216 colors that are available on all Web browsers regardless of the platform used.

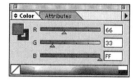

You will notice that even though the sliders are marked with the letters R, G, and B, there are small breaks, or marks, in the sliders; you are confined to choosing colors that lie on those marks.

Combining Shapes

It's possible to create more complex shapes by combining simpler shapes. This is one of the strengths of an illustration program such as Illustrator. You can draw complex shapes using the pen tool, but it would be cumbersome and time consuming. It would certainly be easier, at least in some cases, to combine several simple shapes into one, more complex, shape.

Combining shapes in Illustrator is accomplished using the Pathfinder palette. This palette is not visible by default. To bring it up, choose Window|Show Pathfinder.

Uniting Shapes

You can combine two or more shapes by selecting the shapes using the Selection tool and clicking on the Unite icon on the Pathfinder palette. Note that the new shape will take on the attributes of the uppermost shape.

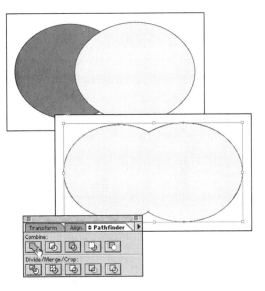

Intersecting Shapes

You can intersect shapes by choosing the shapes using the Selection tool and clicking on the Intersect icon on the Pathfinder palette. Doing this leaves you with a shape that shares the same space as all of the selected shapes. Note that the new shape will have the attributes of the uppermost selected shape.

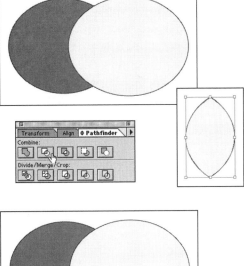

Excluding Shapes

Excluding shapes is the opposite of intersecting shapes. You exclude shapes by choosing the shapes using the Selection tool and clicking on the Exclude icon on the Pathfinder palette. The space shared by the shapes is removed, leaving only the shape of the area where the original shapes did not share space. Note that the new shape will have the attributes of the uppermost selected shape.

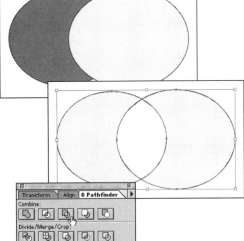

Subtracting from Shapes

You can subtract one shape from another using either Minus Front or Minus Back. If you use Minus Front, the underlying object retains its own attributes and has the overlapping area removed. If you use Minus Back, the upper-most image keeps its attributes while having the underlying shape removed where the two shapes overlap.

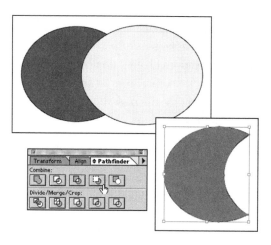

Distorting and Transforming

Illustrator enables you to change the shape of objects. There are a great many possibilities. You can change an object's size and shape and rotate it by making a choice from the Transform menu, but it is even simpler to use the Rotate tool, the Scale tool, and the Free Transform tool from the Toolbox to distort your objects. This allows you to push and pull your objects into weird and wonderful new shapes.

Rotating an Object

You can rotate an object (or group of objects) by choosing it with the Selection tool and then selecting the Rotate tool. When you select the Rotate tool, you'll see a small icon appear in the center of your selected object. This is the center of the rotation icon, which you can place anywhere. Then drag your selected object so that it rotates around the center icon.

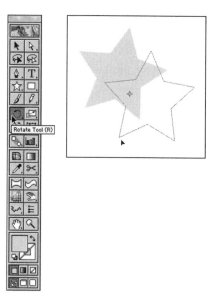

Scaling an Object

You can scale an object (or group of objects) using the Scale tool. To do so, choose the object using the Selection tool and then choose the Scale tool. Place the mouse pointer over the object and click and drag to rescale it.

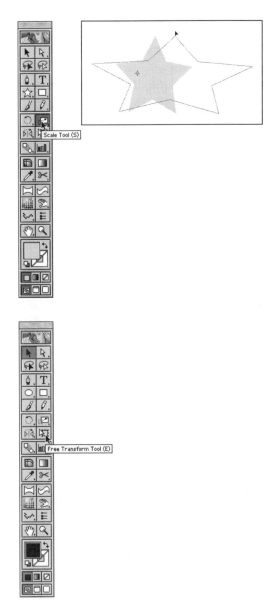

Changing an Object's Shape

You can distort an object's shape in a number of ways. You can shear an object, reflect it, or even change its perspective. All of these distortions can be achieved using the Free Transform tool and a couple of modifier keys.

Shearing an Object

Shearing an object moves its sides in opposite directions. To shear an object (or group of objects), choose it with the Selection tool, and then select the Free Transform tool and click and drag on a side handle (not a corner handle). While you're dragging, hold down the Ctrl and Alt keys on a PC or Option and Command keys on a Mac. You can also add the Shift key to constrain the angle to multiples of 45 degrees. This will add shear to the selected objects.

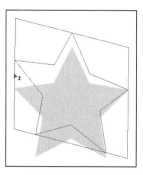

Reflecting an Object

You can also reflect an object (or group of objects). To do so, choose it with the Selection tool, and then select the Free Transform tool and click and drag one of the handles in the direction you want the object to be reflected.

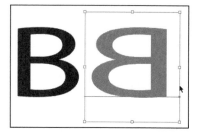

Adding Perspective to an Object

Perspective is one of the most fun distortions you can apply to an object.

To apply perspective to a selected object (or group of objects), select the Free Transform tool and, while holding down the Shift-Ctrl-Alt keys on a PC or Shift-Option-Command keys on a Mac, drag one of the corner handles. You can experiment with dragging in various directions to create different distortions of your object.

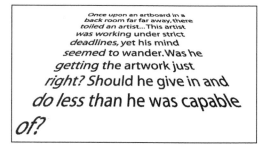

Once upon an artboard in a back room far far away, there toiled an artist... This artist was working under strict deadlines, yet his mind seemed to wander. Was he getting the artwork just right? Should he give in and do less than he was capable of?

Rasterizing Your Vectors

Although vector art has many powerful properties, there may be times when you want your vector artwork transformed to bitmap format. For example, you may want to apply an effect to your artwork that will work only if the artwork is in bitmap format.

Transforming your vector-based artwork into a bitmap is fairly easy. Be aware, though, that this is a one-way process. You can go from vector to bitmap, but not back to vector.

Technically, you can go back to vector using a pro-gram such as Adobe Streamline, but it's never easy to go from bitmap to vector and get good results.

Previewing Vectors as Bitmaps

You can preview your artwork as bitmapped before taking the plunge and changing it. To do so, choose View|Pixel Preview. This will show all of your objects as bitmaps. You will notice the difference more clearly if you zoom in on your artwork.

Setting the Bitmap Options

You may have noticed that the preview option calls bitmaps *pixels* and that the conversion menu calls them *rasters*. Bitmaps, pixels, and rasters are all one and the same. They are just different ways of referring to the way images are displayed on a computer screen.

Several options can be set before rasterizing your vector objects. To see the available options, choose Effect|Rasterize|Raster Effects Settings to bring up the Raster Effects Settings dialog box.

You can set the color mode, as discussed earlier in this chapter, the resolution, the background color, whether the artwork should be anti-aliased, and if it should have a clipping mask.

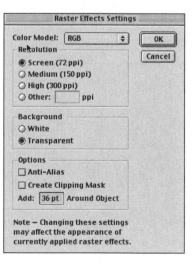

Turning a Vector into a Bitmap

After setting the various options, you can convert your vector artwork to pixels by selecting the object(s) you want to convert using the Selection tool and choosing Effect|Rasterize| Rasterize. You can see the effect of the change by zooming in on your artwork. The bitmap objects will not be as smooth as the vector-based objects.

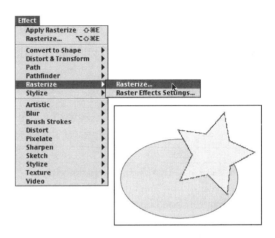

Stylizing Your Objects

Fortunately, with Illustrator 9, you don't have to rasterize your artwork to apply some of the more popular effects (known as *styles* in Illustrator). You can apply effects, such as drop shadows and glows, while keeping the benefits of vector-based artwork. (Please note, however, that some effects in Illustrator work only on bitmaps, others work on vectors, and still others will rasterize the artwork before applying the filter.)

Drop Shadows and Glows

Drop shadows and glows are much sought-after effects. Before Illustrator 9, you'd have to create your artwork and then export/import it into a paint program, such as Adobe Photoshop, to apply these types of effects. This is no longer true. You can now add these popular effects directly to your artwork in Illustrator while keeping the benefits of vector-based objects, such as changing an object's size or shape.

Applying a Drop Shadow

Drop shadows are used to give the illusion of depth to objects. Without a shadow, your artwork can look a little flat. Adding a drop shadow can give the effect of having your objects hover over the background.

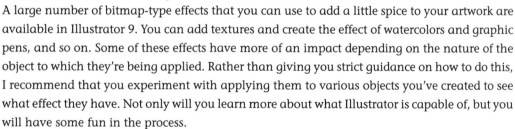

To add a drop shadow, choose the object (or group of objects) you want to apply the effect to using the Selection tool and choose Effect| Stylize|Drop Shadow.

You can adjust the settings for the Mode, Opacity, X and Y Offset, Blur, Color, and Darkness. You can also see a real-time preview of the effect while you work.

Applying a Glow

Glows can give the effect of an object having a neon glow. To add a glow effect to an object (or group of objects), choose the object using the Selection tool and then choose Effect| Stylize|Outer Glow or Inner Glow.

You can adjust the settings for the Mode, Opacity, Blur, and Color of the glow. You can also see a real-time preview of the effect while you work.

Applying Bitmap Effects

A large number of bitmap-type effects that you can use to add a little spice to your artwork are available in Illustrator 9. You can add textures and create the effect of watercolors and graphic pens, and so on. Some of these effects have more of an impact depending on the nature of the object to which they're being applied. Rather than giving you strict guidance on how to do this, I recommend that you experiment with applying them to various objects you've created to see what effect they have. Not only will you learn more about what Illustrator is capable of, but you will have some fun in the process.

Chapter 8
Actions

- Use Illustrator actions

- Run existing actions

- Create actions

- Save and share actions

Using Illustrator Actions

Actions are simply sets of timesaving Illustrator instructions or steps. Illustrator comes with some built-in actions that you can use right out of the box. Even better, though, you can actually create your own actions as simply as performing the series of steps required to create a certain effect or technique. By recording the steps as you perform them, you can save those steps and then replay them at a later date. You can even share the actions you create with others by giving them a copy of the action file you saved.

Exploring the Illustrator Actions Palette

Illustrator actions are accessed using the Action palette. To see this, choose Window|Show Actions, which will reveal the Actions palette. It normally resides beside the Layers and Links palettes.

My Action palette contains a third-party filter, called FILTERiT. If you don't have this filter package, you won't see it listed in your menu selection.

The Actions Palette

The Actions palette is fairly simple. In the main window, you can see a listing of the available sets and actions. To the left of the main window, you can see a couple of icons: The checkmark is an indication of whether or not the action has been toggled on or off, and the small icon that resembles a menu is an indicator of whether the modal control is on or off. Next to the action name is a small arrow icon. This indicates that more steps are available in the action.

A small folder icon, such as the one labeled "Default Actions," indicates that it is a set of actions. A small, black, arrow icon in the upper-right corner of the palette triggers the Actions palette pull-down menu.

The Actions Palette Menu

From within the Actions palette pull-down menu, you can create a new set of actions, and you can duplicate, delete, and play actions. You can also control the creation process. Selections are available that enable you to clear, reset, load, replace, and save actions. And finally, you can also set the Actions palette display mode and you can run batch actions.

Default Mode

Two display modes exist for the Actions palette. The default mode shows information such as whether the action is on or off and whether the modal control is on or off. With the default display on, you can also see the individual steps in an action. You can see the stop, play, and record buttons along the bottom of the palette.

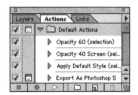

Button Mode

You can set the display mode to button. This displays the actions as buttons that can be clicked on to run any one of the available actions. This mode is great for pointing and clicking on an action.

Running Illustrator Actions

Running an action is pretty much a matter of clicking on the action if the display is set to a button or selecting the action and clicking on the play button.

Some actions may require that a selection be made. If this is the case, simply choose the object (or group of objects) to which you wish to apply the action using the Selection tool, and run the desired action.

Default Actions

Many great actions are available in Illustrator. Some of these are listed under the default set, which is loaded when you install Illustrator. More actions are available, though, on the Application CD-ROM. These "extra" actions can be loaded from the CD and will remain available thereafter.

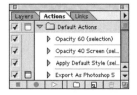

Loading Actions

Loading actions, whether those available as extras on the CD-ROM or from another source, is fairly straightforward. To load a set of actions, simply choose Load Actions from the Actions palette pull-down menu. This will bring up the Load Set From: dialog box.

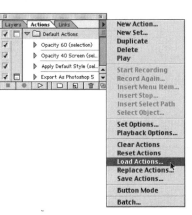

Locate the Actions

To load a set of actions, you must first locate the Actions file. To do so, browse to the Action Sets file from within the Load Set From: dialog box and choose the file. Then click on the Open button. This will load the actions into Illustrator, where they will remain available until you remove them.

One of the Action Sets you may want to load if you create Web graphics is the Buttons set. This set contains several actions that will create different 3D buttons with a click of the mouse.

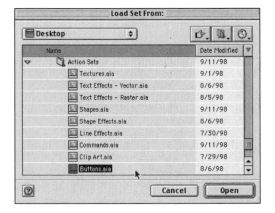

Applying an Action

For the most part, applying an action is as simple as clicking on the Actions button or selecting the action name and clicking on the play button.

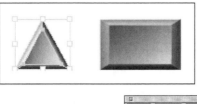

For example, creating a 3D button can be done by selecting the type of button you want to draw from the Actions palette and then simply clicking on the play button at the bottom of the Actions palette.

Running Actions in a Batch

You can even run actions in a batch. This means that you can apply an action to a collection of files. Doing so saves you a lot of time.

Selecting and Applying a Batch Action

To apply a batch action, select Batch from the Actions palette pull-down menu. Doing so brings up the Batch dialog box.

Choosing a Set and an Action

The first thing you should do to run a batch action is to choose a set, and an action from that set, from within the Play option.

Selecting a Source Folder

Next you need to select the source folder. This is the folder that contains the files on which you want to run the action.

Selecting a Destination Folder

You can either Save And Close the files that are changed by the action or you can choose to write them to a new file folder.

Deciding What to Do About Errors

When errors occur, you can either have the action stop or you can have it continue and log the errors to a log file.

Creating Actions

Many powerful built-in actions are available in Illustrator, but the real fun comes from creating and using your own actions. Creating actions is only slightly more complicated than running them. To create an action, you simply need to record the steps you took to create an effect.

To see how easy it is to create an action, follow along with these steps to create an action that will create a daisy with the click of a mouse.

Creating a New Action Set

You can save your actions in existing sets; if this is your first action, however, or if you want to save an action in a new set, you must first create the set. To do this, choose New Set from the Actions palette pull-down menu.

Name the New Action Set

In the New Set dialog box, give your action set a name.

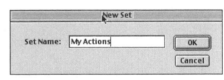

Creating a New Action

Before you can start recording the steps to create your action, you must tell Illustrator to create a new action. To do so, choose New Action from the Actions palette pull-down menu.

Name the New Action

Give your action a descriptive name. Remember that all you will see in the Actions palette is the name you've given the action. I'll call this one Flower, since that's what it will create when it's run.

Recording the Action

After entering a name for the action, you can click on the Record button to start the recording process.

Set the Default Fill and Stroke

Click on the Default Fill and Stroke icon in the Toolbox to set the default white fill and black stroke.

Draw an Ellipse

Select the Ellipse tool and draw an ellipse. This will represent one of the petals of the daisy.

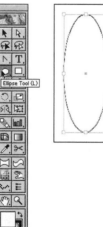

Copy the Ellipse

Choose Edit|Copy to copy the ellipse to the clipboard.

Edit	
Undo Copy	⌘Z
Redo	⇧⌘Z
Cut	⌘X
Copy	**⌘C**
Paste	⌘V
Paste In Front	⌘F
Paste In Back	⌘B
Clear	
Select All	⌘A
Deselect All	⇧⌘A
Select	▶
Define Pattern...	
Edit Original	
Assign Profile...	
Color Settings...	
Keyboard Shortcuts...	⌥⇧⌘K
Preferences	▶

Paste the Ellipse in Front

Choose Edit|Paste In Front to create a second identical ellipse or petal.

Edit	
Undo Copy	⌘Z
Redo	⇧⌘Z
Cut	⌘X
Copy	⌘C
Paste	⌘V
Paste In Front	**⌘F**
Paste In Back	⌘B
Clear	
Select All	⌘A
Deselect All	⇧⌘A
Select	▶
Define Pattern...	
Edit Original	
Assign Profile...	
Color Settings...	
Keyboard Shortcuts...	⌥⇧⌘K
Preferences	▶

Move the Ellipse

Using the Selection tool, move the copy of the ellipse directly below the first ellipse.

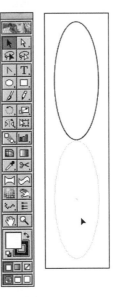

Select Both Ellipses

Using the Selection tool, draw a marquee around both ellipses to select them.

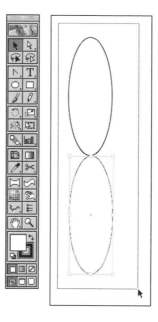

Insert Select Path

From the Actions palette pull-down menu, choose Insert Select Path. This step is necessary since this is the only way to select the path and have that command show up in the action.

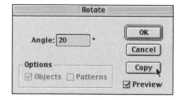

Rotate the Selected Ellipse

Choose Object|Transform|Rotate. Set the angle to 20 degrees and click on the Copy button. This will rotate a copy of the petals.

Stop Recording

Press the Stop Playing/Recording button at the bottom of the Actions palette to stop the recording. At this point, it is necessary to get the action to duplicate the Rotate command and, although you could just repeat the command several times, it is easier to stop the recording and duplicate the command via the Actions palette.

Duplicate the Rotate Command

Duplicate the Rotate command by dragging and dropping it onto the Create New Action icon. This may not make sense, but it actually duplicates the command that you drag, even though it could be used to create or copy an action.

Make eight copies of the command so that you have nine in all.

Play the Action

At this point, you can select and remove all of the objects and then click on the Play Current Selection icon at the bottom of the Actions palette to test your action before proceeding. You should see all of the petals of the daisy appear, as if by magic, before your eyes.

Start Recording

Start recording again by clicking on the Begin Recording icon at the bottom of the Actions palette.

Draw Another Ellipse

Select the Ellipse tool and, while holding down the Alt and Shift keys on a PC or the Option and Shift keys on a Mac, draw another smaller ellipse in the center of the petals. This will be the center of the daisy.

Set the Fill Color

Set the Fill color to a bright yellow and click on the Stop Playing/Recording button again. That's it, you're done! You've just created your first action.

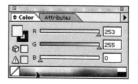

Test Your Action

Select and delete all objects from your artboard. Choose the Flower entry in the Actions palette and click on the Play Current Selection to have Illustrator draw a new daisy almost like magic.

Saving an Action

You should save your action before continuing. You can't actually save the action itself, though; you must save the set. To do so, choose the set from the Actions palette. This should be the set you created at the beginning of this exercise. With the set selected, choose Save Actions from the Actions palette pull-down menu.

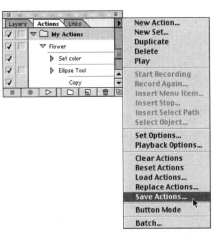

Filing It Away

Browse to a folder where you'd like to save the action set. A good location is the same place where Illustrator stores its own actions.

Sharing Your Actions

To share your actions with your friends or to place them on the Internet so others can download them from your Web site, simply copy the Action file to your friends' systems, FTP the file to your Web site, or attach the file to an email.

Chapter 9
Playing with Type

- Add type

- Use different fonts and styles

- Position and align type

- Add effects to type

- Place type on a path

Using Type in Illustrator

Many illustrations use type. You can add type to a birthday card, a brochure, or posters that you create in Illustrator. You can add paragraph type, headlines, captions, and so on. In fact, adding type to an illustration is something that Illustrator enables you to do easily and creatively.

Illustrator gives you amazing control. You can change the kerning, leading, font, size, and more. You can outline type and fill it with patterns and images, as you saw in Chapter 6. Using Illustrator's filters, you can add all kinds of effects to your type. You can even place type into a nonlinear path, such as a circle.

Adding Type

Although a seemingly endless number of type options are available to you in Illustrator, adding type is as easy as selecting the Type tool and clicking (to add character type) or clicking and dragging (to add paragraph type) within the image. (If the terms *character type* and *paragraph type* are confusing, read on. These will soon become clear.)

Once you've added the type, the fun begins. This chapter will show you how to add some pizzazz to your type in Illustrator.

Adding Character Type

To add character type to your image, select the Type tool and click on the image where you want the text placed. It's not too important where you click, though, because you can easily move the type anywhere you like. After clicking with the Type tool, type in your text.

Most of the character type options are available through the Character palette. To view this, choose Type|Character. From the Character palette, you can select a font family and then set the font's style, size, and spacing. These options will be explained later in this chapter.

Adding Paragraph Type

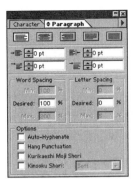

Adding paragraph type is almost as simple as adding character type. To add paragraph type to your image, select the Type tool and click and drag a rectangular shape. This area is where your text will be entered. Then type in the text you want to enter.

You'll find some helpful paragraph type options available in the Paragraph palette. To view this, choose Type|Paragraph from the menu. Using the options in the Paragraph palette, you can set the alignment of your type and change the spacing between words and letters.

Fonts, Sizes, and Spacing

You can use Illustrator to type text in any font you have available on your system. You can scale the type using the Selection tool as you would with any other vector object, or you can set precise point sizes. You can also set exact spacing between characters and between lines of type.

Using text in Illustrator is an exercise in flexibility. In fact, an almost overwhelming number of choices and options are available.

Choosing a Font Family

You can choose a font family before or after typing your text by selecting the existing text using the Type tool or by selecting the text with the Selection tool. You can choose from any font available on your system, and you can set the font from the Type menu or from the Character palette.

Choosing a Font Using the Menus

To choose a font from the Type menu, choose Type|Font and make a choice from the menu. If more fonts are available than fit on the screen, the topmost choice will be labeled "More." Choosing this will offer up more of the available fonts.

Choosing a Font Using the Character Palette

To choose a font from the Character palette, click on the small arrow icon to the right of the Font option. Doing so will reveal a scrolling pull-down menu listing all available fonts. Note that the fonts presented here are reflective of the fonts on my system, and your listings will probably vary.

Choosing a Style

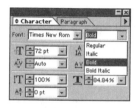

After choosing the font you wish to use, you can set the style. Different styles are available, such as bold and italic. The style available will depend on the font chosen, since some fonts have limited styles. To set the style of a font, click on the small arrow icon next to the style option in the Character palette and choose the desired style from the pull-down menu.

Font Spacing

Many spacing options are available for you to use. You can set the kerning (the amount of space between any two characters), the tracking (the spacing between all selected characters), and the leading (the spacing between lines of type).

Kerning

Kerning sets the spacing between two characters, and adjusting the kerning makes some pairs of characters look more attractive. To set the kerning, select the Type tool and click between the two characters whose kerning you want to adjust. With the cursor in place, choose a new setting from the Character palette. Positive numbers push the two characters further apart, and negative numbers bring them closer together.

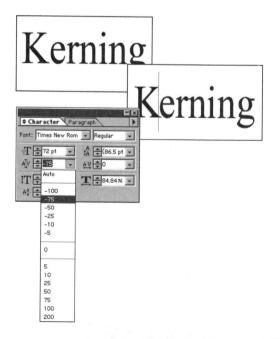

Tracking

Tracking is similar to kerning, but it applies to a range of characters and changes the distance between them equally. Changing the tracking value can be helpful with characters in certain font sets that would otherwise overlap.

To change the tracking, either select the characters using the Type tool or select the entire type object using the Selection tool. With the characters selected, set the new tracking value by changing the number in the Tracking option in the Character palette. You can choose from several preset values or enter a number yourself. Positive values increase the distance between characters, and negative values decrease the distance.

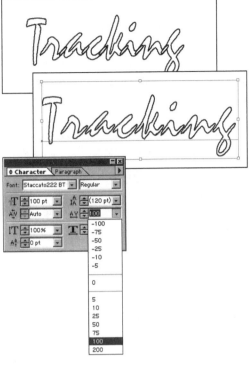

Leading

Leading (pronounced *ledding*) is a term that comes from the days when typesetters placed thin slivers of lead between lines of type. Thicker lead, or more pieces, would increase the spacing.

Today, using Illustrator, you merely need to change the leading value in the Character palette to increase or decrease the spacing between lines of type. To change the leading for a block of type, choose the type object using the Selection tool and change the leading value in the Character palette. Higher numbers increase the space, and lower numbers decrease it. You can actually make lines of type overlap by using low enough values.

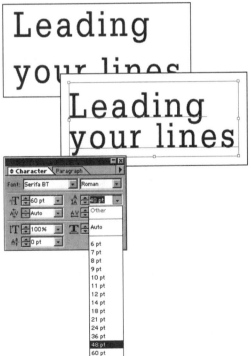

Font Sizing

Because type is a vector object, you can easily change its size by selecting it and clicking and dragging one of its control handles. You can also change the size of your type with more precision, using the controls in the Character palette. In this way, you can change the horizontal and vertical sizes separately and with numerical precision.

Vertical Spacing

You can set the vertical size, or scale, of type using the Vertical Scale option in the Character palette. To set the vertical size of some type, choose the type using the Selection tool and choose a value from the Vertical Scale option pull-down menu, or type in a new value in the option field.

If you don't see the Vertical control in the Character palette, click on the arrow icon in the upper-right corner of the palette and choose Show Options.

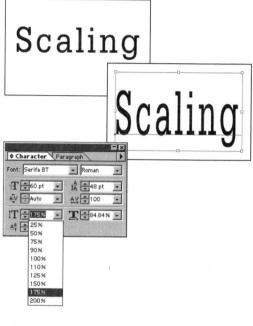

Horizontal Spacing

You can set the horizontal size, or scale, of type using the Horizontal Scale option in the Character palette. To set the horizontal size of some type, choose the type using the Selection tool and choose a value from the Horizontal Scale option pull-down menu, or type in a new value in the option field.

If you don't see the Horizontal control in the Character palette, click on the arrow icon in the upper-right corner of the palette and choose Show Options.

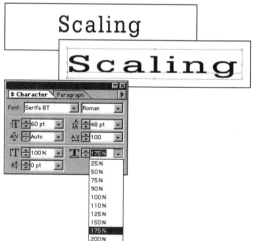

Positioning and Aligning Your Type

You can use many different settings and options when positioning your type in Illustrator. You can adjust the baseline shift; align the type left, center, or right; or even fully justify it.

Baseline Shift

When you enter text with the Type tool, the text is placed along an invisible line known as the *baseline*. You can adjust how your type interacts with the baseline, placing it above, below, or along that line.

To change the baseline shift of any type, choose the type with the Selection tool. To select a portion of a block of type, use the Type tool to select only the type you want. With the type selected, you can move it above the baseline by entering a positive number in the Baseline Shift option in the Character palette. Similarly, you can move the type below the baseline by entering a negative number.

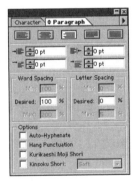

Justifying Type

Justifying type changes how lines of text line up with each other. You can align type to the left or right, center it, or even justify it. You will find the alignment and justification options in the Paragraph palette. To see all the options available in the Paragraph palette, choose Type|Paragraph and click on the small arrow icon in the upper-right corner of the palette and choose Show Options.

Align Left

To align type to the left, choose the type using the Selection tool and then click on the Align Left icon in the Paragraph palette.

Align Center

To center type, choose the type using the Selection tool and then click on the Align Center icon in the Paragraph palette.

Align Right

To align type to the right, choose the type using the Selection tool and then click on the Align Right icon in the Paragraph palette.

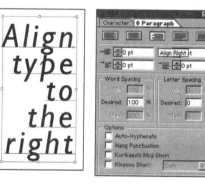

Justifying Full Lines

To justify full lines of type, choose the type using the Selection tool and then click on the Justify Full Lines icon in the Paragraph palette.

To justify full lines of type select the type you want justified using the Selection tool and then click the Justify Full Lines icon in the Paragraph palette.

Justifying All Lines

To justify all lines of type, choose the type using the Selection tool and then click on the Justify All Lines icon in the Paragraph palette.

To justify all lines of type select the type you want justified using the Selection tool and then click the Justify Full Lines icon in the Paragraph palette.

Adding Effects to Type

You can use many of the same types of effects on type in Illustrator as you do with any other vector object. Type is a little different, though, in that it remains editable and you can do certain tasks to it, such as spell-check it.

In previous versions of Illustrator, there were occasions where you would need to convert type to curves before applying certain effects. Once converted, it was not possible to edit the type further. This is no longer true. You can now apply many effects to type and still change the text afterwards. The next section describes this and introduces you to applying effects to your type.

Adding a Gaussian Blur Effect to Type

The Gaussian blur effect has been used quite a bit in magazines, Web sites, and even many television ads. The effect places type, enlarged and blurred, behind the same, smaller, sharper type. It's easy to reproduce this effect; in Illustrator 9, you can even edit the blurred type. To see how this effect is accomplished, complete the following steps.

Open a New File and Add Type

Open a new file by choosing File|New. Select the Type tool and choose a font from the Character palette. Enter the words "Gausian Blur". Note the deliberate misspelling. We'll fix this in a later step to prove that the type remains fully editable. I chose Gill Sans as the font and Regular as the type. I'll change this later, too.

Color the Type

With the type entered, you can change its color. To do this, choose the type using the Selection tool and adjust the color in the Color palette. I set the color to a light gray and used 200 as the value for the Red, Green, and Blue.

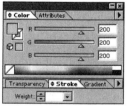

Resize the Type

I want the type to be much larger, but I don't have any specific size in mind. I just want the type to fill most of the horizontal width of the artboard. To enlarge the type, choose it using the Selection tool and then resize it by clicking and dragging one of the corner control points.

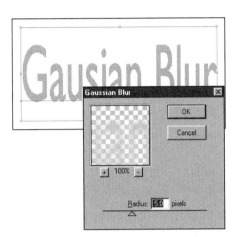

Apply the Gaussian Blur Effect

To apply the Gaussian Blur effect, choose the type with the Selection tool, if it's not already selected, and choose Effect|Blur|Gaussian Blur. Set the Radius to 5.0 to get a good blur.

Correct the Misspelling

Oops, I just noticed a spelling error. With previous versions of Illustrator, this would have meant having to start over. With Illustrator 9, though, it's a simple matter of selecting the Type tool, placing it over the text, and clicking and entering the change. Note how the type remains at the same size and color, and with the effects intact.

Change the Font Style

Suppose the art director shows up after you've created the artwork, effects and all, and decides that the font style should be changed to bold italic or that the font should be different. No problem!

To change the font family or the style, choose the type using the Selection tool, if it's not already selected, and simply choose the new font or style from the Character palette.

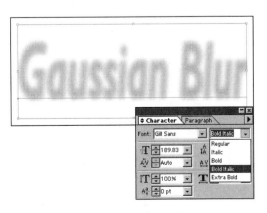

Apply the Finishing Touch

To add the finishing touch, add the same text in 48 point type and move it into place. I used black as the color of the type, but you can choose a color to suit the work you're doing.

Type on a Path

One of the most sought-after effects is that of placing type along a path. Many people want to be able to place type around a circle, for example. Unfortunately, they usually encounter problems because they try to do this using a paint program, such as Photoshop, when they need a vector-based drawing program like Illustrator.

Creating Type on a Path

Creating type on a path, even a circle, is quite easy using Illustrator. I'll show you how to create type on a curved path in three steps, but you can use exactly the same method to add type to circular, rectangular, or star-shaped paths, or any other type of path you choose.

Create a New File and Add the Path

To create a curved path similar to mine, drawn using the Pen tool, click and drag in an upward direction. Release the mouse button, move the pointer to the right, and then click and drag downwards. Doing so will create a nice flowing curve. You can also create a shape using the Ellipse or the Rectangle tool.

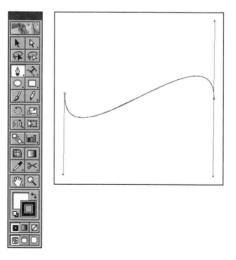

Select the Type on a Path Tool

Select the Path Type tool and place the mouse pointer somewhere on the path you've drawn.

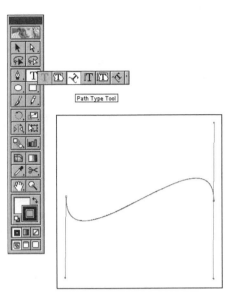

Add the Type

Click on the mouse button to add the type along the path. If you get an error dialog box, you haven't clicked directly on the path. If this happens, simply clear the dialog box by clicking on OK and try again. You'll notice that I adjusted the curve of my path, which I did using the Direct Selection tool, as explained in Chapter 5.

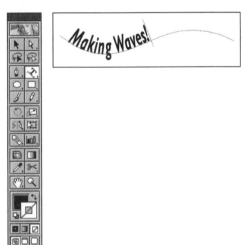

Modify the Type

Depending on the path and the type, you may want to modify the type—to resize it, for example. To do so, simply select the type using the Type tool and then make the appropriate changes in the Character palette. If necessary, you can adjust the kerning or tracking, or make any other modifications to your type using the knowledge you've gained from this chapter.

Chapter 10
Illustrator for the Web

- Use Web-safe colors

- Rasterize images

- Export graphics for the Web

- Create image maps

Creating Web Graphics with Illustrator

Although many people favor using a paint program or photo-editing program such as Photoshop for editing graphics and images intended for the Web, Illustrator is the perfect tool for creating Web graphics. You've already seen how to use the various shape and drawing tools in Illustrator. These tools make creating Web graphics a snap.

Illustrator, like all graphics programs, contains tools that can help you design and create graphics for your Web pages. Whether you need backgrounds, buttons, or an entire interface, Illustrator is a great choice.

Setting Up for Web Graphics

Planning the size of the Web-destined images may seem obvious, but I've seen many designers start creating graphics destined for the Web without giving any thought to their final size.

Many designers use fairly powerful systems with large screens at high resolution (many use a resolution higher than 800×600 pixels). Designing buttons or other graphics intended to be displayed in a Web browser running on a user's monitor set to a resolution of 640×480 pixels can be a problem.The resulting graphics tend to be too large when displayed on most systems. There is an easy solution, though. Simply set the artboard size appropriately when you create a new file. This will give you an idea of how the graphic will fit in the browser window.

Setting the Artboard Size and Color Mode

To set the artboard to a more appropriate size, set the Width to 600 points and the Height to 400 points. If the browser is set to 640×480, my settings of 600×400 should work nicely since various borders and menus take up some of the space of the browser. Remember that the size is chosen to give you a visual reference.

Because computer monitors display colors using RGB (Red, Green, and Blue), you should also set the Color Mode to RGB Color.

Previewing the Correct Size

To see the actual size of the artboard, you can double-click on the Zoom tool. This will force the artboard to display at the size you've chosen. Note that, if your own screen resolution is set to 640×480, the artboard edges may not be visible.

Now, when you draw the various shapes and lines as you create your Web graphics, you'll have a good idea of how they'll appear in the average browser window.

Web-Safe Colors

One of the most common problems Web designers have is using colors that appear as close as possible to the original color, no matter what system the user has.

It is easier for most users' systems to use a set of colors known as Web-safe or browser-safe colors. This set contains 216 colors. This can be limiting, to be sure, and it's a real challenge to create great graphics using such a limited palette. Fortunately, Illustrator helps when it comes to setting and changing colors suited for the Web.

Setting Web-Safe Colors with the Color Palette

You can set Web-safe colors using the Color Palette. To do so, simply click the small arrow icon in the upper right corner of the palette (choose Window|Show Color to view the Color palette) to bring up the pull-down menu, and choose Web Safe RGB. Choosing colors from the palette with this setting will allow you to pick only Web-safe colors.

Setting Web-Safe Colors with the Color Picker Dialog Box

You can also choose Web-safe colors from the Color Picker dialog box. To do so, double-click on either the Fill or Stroke icon in the Toolbox to bring up this dialog box. With the dialog box active, place a checkmark in the Only Web Colors option. This will display only Web-safe colors from which to choose as you design your graphics.

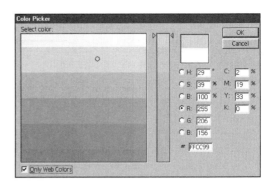

Converting an Object's Color Mode

If you've already created your graphic and it contains objects drawn in color modes other than Web-safe colors, Illustrator allows you to convert the color mode. To do so, complete the following steps.

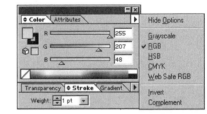

Select an Object

Before you can convert the color mode of an object, you must select the object. To do so, simply choose the Selection tool and click on the object.

Change the Color Mode

With the object selected, set the color mode to Web Safe RGB. This will, of course, cause some color shifting. This will be more noticeable with gradients.

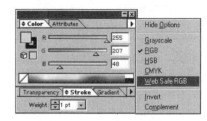

Possible Problems

You will experience problems when trying to convert several objects at once or when trying to convert gradients to Web-safe colors. Illustrator will simply convert the objects to a default setting, such as white fill and black stroke. To get around this problem, you may want to convert objects one at a time and limit the use of gradients.

Vectors versus Pixels

Images created with Illustrator are vector based. That is, they are described mathematically. When you resize an object, the math is simply changed and the object is redisplayed. This keeps objects looking sharp on screen and when printed.

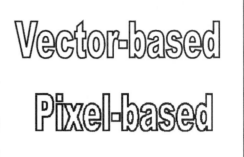

By their nature, objects displayed on a computer screen are pixel based. This means that they are made up of a collection, or array, of pixels of varying colors. When you view your images in Illustrator, they are vector based. Images exported as Web graphics will be pixel based, or bitmapped (also known as raster images). This might seem problematic. However, Illustrator offers a great solution: You can preview images in pixel mode.

Previewing in Pixel Mode

With Illustrator, you can preview what your images will look like when you finally rasterize them. Then you will know what the final image will look like in a Web browser. To preview your image in pixel mode, choose View|Pixel Preview. This option is a toggle, meaning that selecting the option will change the view to pixel mode, and selecting it again will return the view to vector mode.

Note that choosing the pixel preview mode doesn't rasterize your image; it simply sets the view to pixel mode.

Rasterizing Your Images

If you're ready to take the plunge, you can rasterize your image. This means that your objects will no longer be manipulated as vectors. Before converting your image to bitmap (discussed in more detail in Chapter 7), you may want to save a copy first or create a duplicate object. Doing so allows you to go back later and make changes to the vector-based objects.

Setting the Raster Options

Before you rasterize your image, you should inspect and set the raster options. To do so, choose Effect|Rasterize|Raster Effects Settings. This brings up the Raster Effects Settings dialog box. Choose a color model, set the resolution (select Screen [72ppi] for Web-based artwork), set the Background, and turn Anti-Alias on to soften the edges of your objects.

Converting an Image to Pixels

With the raster options properly set, you can rasterize your image. To do so, choose all of the objects you want rasterized using the Selection tool and then choose Effect|Rasterize|Rasterize. This brings up the Raster Effects Settings dialog box. Because you've preset the options, though, you can simply click OK to apply the change.

If you try zooming in on your image using the Zoom tool, you'll notice the difference between the rasterized version and the vector-based version.

Exporting Graphics for the Web

Of course, the reason you've applied Web-safe colors and rasterized your artwork is so you can export it in a file format compatible with Web browsers. For now, you're limited to JPEG and GIF.

Exporting JPEG Files

Much of the artwork you create in Illustrator is best exported as GIF files for use on the Web. There will be times, however, when you create images—with gradients, for example—that best lend themselves to being exported as JPEG files.

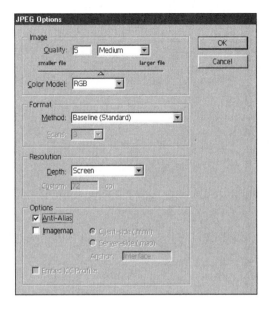

To export a JPEG file, choose File|Export and choose JPEG (*.JPG) from the Save As pull-down menu. This brings up the JPEG Options dialog box. You can use the settings in this dialog box to set the various JPEG file options. You can set the image quality. Higher values mean larger file sizes and, subsequently, longer download times. Web designers must strike a balance between using better quality and larger image sizes with the possibility of losing Web site visitors because of long download times.

Leave the Color Model set to RGB. You can also leave the default settings for the Format and Resolution.

If you want the image to have softer, smoother edges, place a checkmark in the Anti-Alias option.

Saving for the Web

Exporting Illustrator files in the GIF format is done by choosing File|Save For Web. This brings up a dialog box with many settings and options that you can use to save your files. One option you can use to great advantage is 4-Up. Choosing 4-Up from the tab across the top of the dialog box gives you four views of your image. You can set these to various views, such as Original, GIF, and JPEG. You are then always able to compare the file sizes and quality of the images in real time.

To set any of the views, simply click one of the images and then set the options along the right side of the dialog box. This view will then adopt those settings, and you can compare it to the other views.

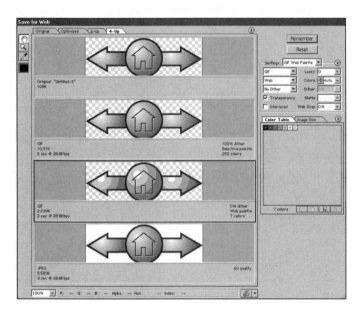

Creating an Image Map

Image maps are images with clickable areas. These images are special kinds of graphics generally used for interfaces on Web pages. The clickable areas can be rectangular, circular, or polygonal. Before this technology was built into programs such as Illustrator, a Web designer had to create image maps by hand. This was long and tedious. With Illustrator, creating an image map is simple.

Building an Image Map

Building an image map takes a few steps. To start out, you should create the image that you'll be using as the image map. This can be accomplished using the various tools and techniques presented throughout this book.

Once you've created an image, follow these steps to create an image map.

Select an Object

Before you can make an object clickable, you must choose it using the Selection tool. Then choose Window|Show Attributes, to bring up the Attributes palette. Within the Attributes palette, you can set the Image Map. Choose from None, Rectangle, or Polygon. You must also set a URL (Uniform Resource Locator) for the object. This should reflect the address of the page that will be linked to the object in the map.

Repeat the process for all objects.

Export the Image

With all of the objects selected and given image map attributes, you are ready to export the image. Choose File|Export, set the file type to JPEG, and give the file a name. Click on OK to bring up the JPEG Options dialog box. In this box, place a checkmark in the Imagemap option. You must also choose a name for the map. This is an arbitrary name that will be used in the resulting HTML (HyperText Markup Language) to identify the map. Click on OK to save the file and write out the HTML. The HTML file will be saved in the same directory and have the same name as the JPEG file. Either of these can be changed later.

You may eventually want to cut and paste from the HTML that Illustrator wrote. Although this is a fairly straightforward process, it's beyond the scope of this book. (If you want to learn more about HTML, see *HTML Black Book* by Steven Holzner [Scottsdale, AZ: The Coriolis Group, 2000].)

Inspect the Image Map

To see your new image map in action, locate the HTML file that Illustrator created (it will be saved in the same folder as the image you saved), and double-click on its icon. This will bring up a Web page with only the image map visible. Moving the mouse over the various objects in the image map will reveal the URL associated with each object in the status bar of the Web browser. You can view the source that Illustrator created—and edit it, of course—by choosing View|Source from the browser menu.

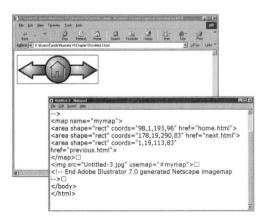

Part II
Projects

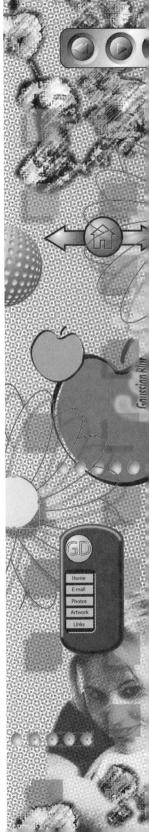

Chapter 11
Coloring Line Art

 Project 1: Scan Your Line Art

 Project 2: Vectorize Your Artwork

 Project 3: Add Color and More

Working with Hand-Drawn Line Art

This chapter introduces you to the techniques of scanning, importing, and re-creating your hand-drawn line art in Illustrator. The first step, discussed in the first project, will be to scan your hand-drawn artwork into Illustrator. To do so, you need to have access to Photoshop and a scanner. In the second project, after you have scanned the artwork into Photoshop, you will use Adobe Streamline to "vectorize" the artwork. And once your hand-drawn artwork has been vectorized, it can be opened and manipulated in Illustrator—as discussed in the final project.

Project 1: Scan Your Line Art

Illustrator is a powerful drawing tool, but there will be times when you need to use artwork that's been created using traditional media such as hand-drawn sketches. The problem is how to get the artwork from the paper into Illustrator where you can manipulate it with all the digital tools Illustrator offers.

Illustrator itself doesn't offer a method to enable you to scan the artwork into the program. For that, you need a photo-editing program such as Adobe Photoshop.

Scan Your Line Art Directly

Using Photoshop, and any TWAIN-compliant scanner (TWAIN stands for Technology Without An Interesting Name), you can easily scan your hand-drawn sketches. The setup will depend on your scanner and its software.

Note that many scanners do in fact come with software that enables you to scan and save your work without using Photoshop or some other image-editing software.

As easy as the process is, though, you need to overcome a couple of hurdles. Just lying your artwork on the scanner and scanning it without any preparation could end up costing you more time.

For example, although a sketch with shading will certainly scan well, it isn't a good candidate for vectorizing. Since you can apply shading, color, and many other effects once you've imported the sketch into Illustrator, you should scan an original image that's clean.

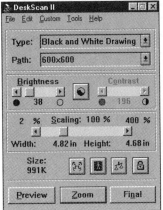

Trace Your Artwork

One easy way to overcome the problem of not having a clean sketch is to make a tracing of your existing sketch. Use a marker or wide-tipped pen to make definite lines that will scan well. Having a dark, lined version of your artwork will make the rest of the process much easier.

Prepare Your Artwork

You may want to prepare your artwork in other ways before scanning it. For example, you should break up certain areas so they'll become separate objects when you turn the scan into a vector-based series of objects, and so they can be imported into Illustrator easily. You'll notice, for example, that I used the Eraser tool, in Photoshop, to break the main object (the apple) and the stem into two separate objects. This is a crucial step. Neglecting to break up the artwork before scanning it will result in more work once you get the artwork into Illustrator.

With all your preparations completed, scan the artwork into Photoshop and save the file using the TIFF (tagged image file format) format.

Project 2: Vectorize Your Artwork

With the artwork scanned and saved, it's time to turn the bitmap art into vector-based artwork. This can be done in several ways, some simpler than others. You can use Illustrator itself, for example, or, if you own Adobe Streamline, you can use that.

Use Adobe Streamline

Using Streamline is the easiest way to create vectors from your artwork. As good as it is, though, it's not perfect. You still need to use the steps outlined in the first project to prepare your artwork. Having done so, though, almost guarantees you a successful port from bitmap to vectors. To vectorize your artwork using Streamline, follow these steps.

1.

With your scanned artwork opened in Streamline, you can clean it up, if necessary. You can, for example, use the Eraser tool to erase any stray marks from the paper or the scan if you didn't already do so in Photoshop.

If you own Streamline and a TWAIN-compliant scanner, you can scan the artwork directly into Streamline.

2.

Several conversion settings can be adjusted in Streamline. The type of artwork you're converting, and the final results you have in mind, will dictate how you convert the image.

For the simple artwork used in this example, I want to have Streamline create a centerline through all of the lines that make up the traced version of the original. I have left most of the other settings at their default.

3.

With the settings adjusted, choose File|Convert to convert the artwork into a series of vector objects. You are then presented with a preview of the converted artwork. If the results are not satisfactory, you can reset some of the conversion options and try again.

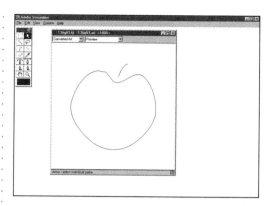

4.

You should end up with a clean vector-based image that can be saved from Streamline as an Illustrator (AI) file. To do so, choose File|Save Art As and give the file a name.

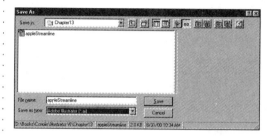

5.

The file you saved in Streamline will open in Illustrator as a series of vector objects. If you used the methods outlined in the previous steps, you will have a vector-based image that you can manipulate easily in Illustrator.

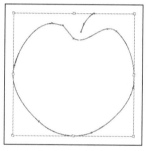

Use Illustrator to Vectorize Artwork

As an alternative, you can use Illustrator's built-in Auto Trace tool to vectorize your bitmap images. The Auto Trace tool is more limited in its functionality than Streamline, but it will work in a pinch. To see how Auto Trace can help you create vector-based objects from your artwork, follow these steps.

1.

Open your artwork in Illustrator. I am using the same TIF file saved from the scan in Photoshop, and I have already cleaned up the artwork and broken up any objects.

Note that you can just open the file and you don't have to Place it.

2.

To trace your bitmap artwork, select the Auto Trace tool and click near the edge of any object you want traced.

On simple objects, such as the outline of the apple sketch, Illustrator's Auto Trace tool does as good a job as Streamline. If you find that you are converting many sketches, though, you may want to invest in Streamline.

3.

Click on any other objects in the bitmap artwork that you want converted. You may find that, unlike Streamline, objects are outlined rather than having centerlines drawn through them. For some shapes, this is not a problem. For others, however, you have to complete some extra steps to get the effect you're after.

4.

In some cases, fixing the problem of not having a centerline drawn through an object will
be a simple matter of selecting the Scissors tool
and cutting the shape into lines that can then
be deleted or modified as necessary.

Depending on what you intend to do with each
object you've created, you may not want to
change the outline to a line. Again, it depends
on what you want to do with the various objects in the artwork.

In my illustration, I've zoomed in on the stem
to make the necessary changes.

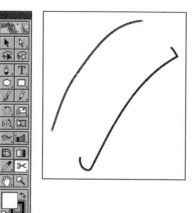

Project 3: Add Color and More

Once you've got all of the objects converted to vectors, you can apply color, edit the lines, change the brush stroke, copy the objects, and more. At this point, you have full access to the powerful vector-based drawing tools that Illustrator has to offer.

Create a Poster from Your Sketch

As an example, I want to create a small poster based on the apple sketch, so I will copy the objects I created, color them, and add a couple of Illustrator effects to get the final artwork I have planned.

1.

To get started on the poster, now that the sketched artwork has been converted to vectors, choose the objects using the Selection tool. Choose Edit|Copy and then Edit|Paste In Front to make a new copy of the objects. Using the Selection tool, move the new objects aside so you can work with them separately.

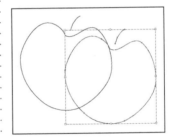

2.

With the new objects still selected, change the brushstroke. I added a stylish stroke to the apple and the stem, and I also changed the fill to none.

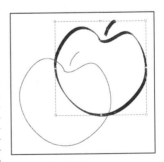

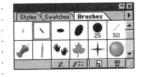

3.

The color object won't need the stem, so you can select it and delete it. Then select the first copy of the apple shape and set the stroke to none and the color to a bright red.

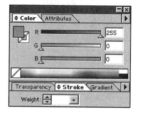

4.

Because I want a nice illustrated effect for the poster, I'll move the stroked shapes over the filled color shape, but I'll leave the stroked shapes offset a little.

5.

Choose all of the shapes using the Selection tool. With the shapes selected, choose Edit|Copy and then Edit|Paste In Front to create another apple and move it to the side. Then select the color object in the new apple and change its color to a bright green.

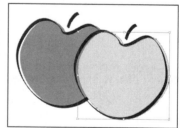

6.

To make the apples appear less clonelike, you can select one of them and rotate it slightly. You can also edit the shape or even change its size. Now that the sketch has been converted to vectors, you can apply any vector tools to it.

In addition to rotating the red apple, I've made it a little smaller so that it appears to be behind the green apple.

7.

I'd like to add a stylish border to the poster, which is easy to do with Illustrator.

To add a border, draw a rectangular shape with a black stroke and no fill color, and set the brushstroke of the rectangle to a stylish paint stroke. You will find many different brush strokes in the Brushes palette.

8.

To add a textured background to the poster, create another rectangle that fills the whole artboard. Set the fill color of the new rectangle to a light beige (I used R: 255; G: 222; B: 172) and set the stroke to none. Move the new rectangle to the back behind all of the other objects by choosing Object|Arrange|Move to Back. To apply the texture, choose Effect|Texture| Texturizer.

I chose to add a canvas effect to give the impression that the poster is painted on a burlap sack.

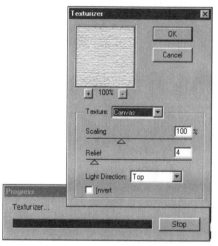

9.

To finalize the poster, select the Type tool and add some type. I used 72pt. Comic Sans MS Bold. I then stretched the type a little using the Selection tool. I also changed the fill color to a medium dark gray and changed the stroke from 1 point to 3 points to make the type stand out.

At this point, if you've followed along and have a similar illustration, you can continue to add, edit, and apply effects to it until you have a finished illustration with results you like.

Chapter 12
Creating a Brochure

Creating Your Own Brochures and Other Business Documents

With the low cost of today's hardware, such as scanners and color inkjet printers, it's a snap to create your own flyers, letterhead, and business cards for your business. This chapter will give you some ideas and show you how to create an eye-catching brochure. Many of these same ideas can be applied to creating other business documents.

Illustrator is the perfect tool to help you create imaginative and inexpensive brochures. Using some of the techniques you've learned in the preceding chapters, you can easily create a stunning business brochure.

Project 1: Plan the Layout

The first thing to do is plan the layout. You may want to sketch out something with a pencil and paper or simply start laying out ideas in Illustrator. It's common today to lay out areas of a brochure using large solid blocks of color.

You can use Illustrator to block out some rough ideas to see how the composition looks.

1.

To get started, select the Rectangle tool and draw a rectangle. Choose Edit|Copy and then Edit|Paste In Front to make a copy of it.

2.

Hold down the Shift key and tap the right-arrow key to move the copied rectangle to the right until it's not touching the first rectangle.

3.

Perform the same copy-and-paste action with the second rectangle and move it to the right as well. You should now have three rectangles lined up in a row.

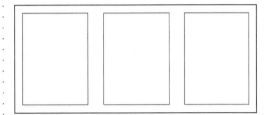

4.

Use the Selection tool to select all three rectangles and copy and paste them in front. Hold down the Shift key and tap the down-arrow key until you have two rows of three rectangles. You now have six rectangles that represent the pages on which you can try your layout ideas.

5.

Select the Rectangle tool again and draw a new rectangle that covers the first third or so of the first rectangle vertically. Click on the Fill icon in the Toolbox and, in the Color palette, change the fill color to a light gray. I used 200 for each of the Red, Green, and Blue values.

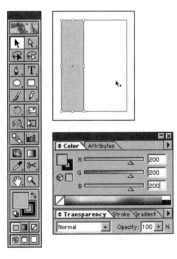

6.

Repeat Step 5, but this time, in the second rectangle, add a horizontal rectangular area.

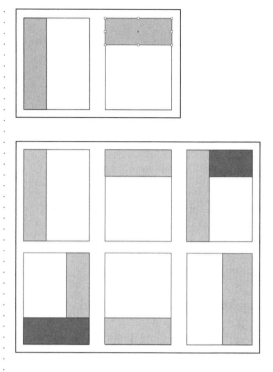

7.

Continue adding gray rectangular areas to the other rectangles. You can add more than one gray area to each, and you can change the shades of gray. You can also change the width and height of the rectangles. At the end of the process, you should have six different layouts to choose from. You can pick one, or you can add more rectangles and add areas to them. Keep adding rectangles or modifying the ones you've created until you have a layout you like. Keep the layout simple and don't add more than two rectangular areas. You can see that I have created six good possibilities just by adding one or two rectangular areas in different places on the rectangles I've drawn.

8.

Choose the one layout that really works for you. Remember that, because all the objects you create in Illustrator are vector based, you can easily move, edit, and resize them at any time. It will therefore be fairly easy to change your mind during the design and creation process.

I've chosen the third layout as the one I'll use. To remove the others, select them and press the Delete key. Select the layout you've chosen and enlarge it by dragging the corners out toward the edges of the artboard.

This is a good time to save the file. To do so, choose File|Save As, browse to the folder you want to save the file in, and give the file a name. I've called mine Layout.ai.

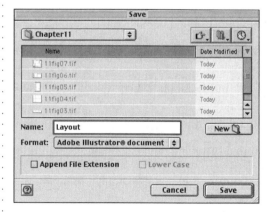

Project 2: Import Photographs and Artwork

Now that you have the main layout prepared, it's time to add some artwork to the brochure. You can add a company logo, for example, or some product photographs.

1.

To add other Illustrator artwork, you can simply open the artwork and copy and paste it into the layout. If you have some vector-based artwork, such as a company logo, use it. You can, of course, use some of what you've learned in the preceding chapters to create some new artwork. But again, don't worry too much about the colors and the placement: Vector-based objects are easily moved, colored, and edited.

You can see that I added a logo to the upper left corner of the artwork. I designed this "eye" logo using shapes, lines, and a blend between a couple of shapes.

2.

To add graphics to the brochure, simply choose File|Place. Browse to the folder containing the graphics, select the graphic, and click on OK. Move the graphic—in this case, a screen capture—into place. Your placement only has to be approximate since you will move the objects around as you finalize the design.

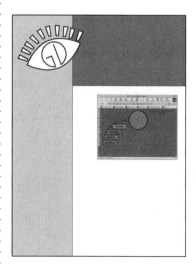

Project 3: Add Type

It's time to add some type to the brochure. I added a company name, using some bold type to give the reader an idea of what the brochure is all about, and I also added some descriptive text for the product/service that I'm marketing.

1.

Select the Type tool and type in the company name. I used the New York typeface at roughly 80 points for the type and I moved the type into place at the top of the brochure. I used this font because I wanted something elegant but at the same time businesslike. Choosing a font can be a difficult process that is beyond the scope of this book. Many good books are available on the subject of typography, though, and you can easily find one at your local library or bookstore, or you can find information online.

2.

I added some text below the company name to be sure that readers know what I'm advertising. I also added a blurb along the side to catch the reader's interest.

Note that the type below the company name is in the same font. I made it smaller and set it well below the company name. I used a different, sans serif, font for the blurb. I chose this font because it's easier to read at a glance.

"Sans serif" refers to not having the serifs on a font. ("Sans" means "without" in French.) Serifs are the decorative ends you see on many fonts, such as Times Roman. A general rule of thumb when it comes to type is: You should rarely use more than three or four different fonts. I'm using one for the company name, another for the blurb, and a third for the descriptive type—that is, the body text.

Project 4: Wrap Type

To add a little flair to the body type, it would be nice to wrap it around the placed graphic. This is possible, but it will require a little work. To enter some body text and wrap it around a placed piece of art, follow these steps:

1.

Temporarily move the placed graphic off the work area. Select the Type tool and click and drag a rectangular area to hold the body text.

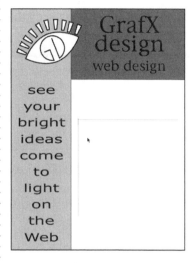

2.

Enter the body text and set the font and the size. I used the same sans serif type as the blurb and set the size to 14 points. (Since this brochure is for a Canadian company, I've used the British spelling of "presense.")

3.

Select the Rectangle tool and draw a rectangle near the upper-right corner of the body type. This rectangle represents the area that the graphic will occupy. The type will wrap around this area, and we'll move the graphic back into place after wrapping the type. The reason we need to create a rectangle in place of the graphic is that Illustrator will not wrap type around placed objects such as graphics. This workaround is fairly simple, though, and it will give us the elegant effect we want.

4.

Use the Selection tool to select both the body text and the rectangle. Note that the rectangle must be in front of the type. If you created them in the same order as I did, this should not be a problem. If your rectangle is behind the type, however, simply choose the rectangle using the Selection tool and choose Object|Arrange|Bring Forward.

5.

To wrap the type around the rectangle, choose Type|Wrap|Make. Doing so will wrap the type around the rectangle. If you don't like the way the type is wrapped, you can undo it using Type|Wrap|Release or by simply choosing Edit|Undo. At this point, you can move the rectangle or resize it and try wrapping the type again until it suits your taste.

6.

Move the placed graphic back into place inside the wrapped type. You may find that you have to resize the graphic. You may also find that you have to arrange the order of the objects so that the graphic is in front of the rectangle the text is wrapped around. If this is the case, simply select the graphic using the Selection tool and choose Object|Arrange|Move to Front.

Project 5: The Final Artwork

Now it's time to polish the brochure. You can move some of the objects around, change some of the type, and have someone proofread the copy. The idea now is to perfect the project to the point where it's ready to be printed and distributed.

1.

I decided to move the "web design" type from the upper rectangle to just below the rectangle and just above the body type. This means that I should move the company name down, as well.

2.

As you finalize your brochure, you may notice a few things that need changing. I decided to rotate the logo a little more. To do so, I chose the logo using the Selection tool and simply rotated it in the direction I wanted.

3.

Of course, clients need to be able to contact you. I added the company URL to the bottom of the brochure using the same type as the body text but in a larger point size.

Most of these same techniques can be used to create letterheads, flyers, posters, and newsletters. You're limited only by your imagination!

see
your
bright
ideas
come
to
light
on
the
Web

GrafX design

web design

At GrafX Design we specialize in helping small businesses create a presense on the Web. We won't just design a website for you, we'll help you understnd the Web and how you can use it to your advantage. We like to get our customers involved in the process and we offer training in how to maintain their websites and how to make good use of search engines. We also advise our clients on how to advertise and market their products/services on the Web. In short, we don't just sell you a website, we sell you a Web-based solution.

www.grafx-design.com

Chapter 13
Effects Tricks

 Project 1: Apply Filters

 Project 2: Apply Bitmap Effects

 Project 3: Use Third-Party Filters

 Project 4: Use Photo Crosshatching Techniques

Using Illustrator's Effects

Using the built-in effects that come with Illustrator, you can create all sorts of illustrations. The following projects will show you how to create a yin-yang symbol from a couple of circular shapes, how to create a painterly effect from a scanned photograph, how to create a realistic golf ball using a couple of spheres and some of the built-in filters, and how to use crosshatching techniques on a scanned photo.

Project 1: Apply Filters

Illustrator is a powerful drawing tool. Sometimes, though, you need more than just powerful drawing tools to create certain effects. You may want to create a shape, for example, that is difficult to draw using only freehand methods. That's where the power of filters and effects comes in.

Illustrator ships with an extensive collection of filters and effects. If you're a Photoshop user, you might recognize some of the effects, such as Gaussian Blur. Most of the filters, though, will be new to you if you're new to illustration software. Although we won't examine all of the filters in this chapter (a whole book could be written on filters alone), we will explore some of them and see what they can offer. One that we'll look at in particular, later in this chapter, is the crosshatch filter. This amazing filter creates a crosshatch illustration from a photograph.

Filters are normally applied to vector objects. You may think that this is a bit restrictive, but you will be amazed at the tricks you can pull off with a few mouse clicks.

Create a Yin-Yang Symbol

When you think about it, the yin-yang symbol, although it may seem simple at first glance, is really quite complex. It is composed of two identical shapes that wrap around each other to form a perfect circle. How exactly is that done? You could draw one of the shapes, copy it, and then try to combine them into the circle, but I think you'd quickly realize how tough a job that would be.

You could also try creating the circle and then drawing a curve down the center. Although this approach might be less time consuming, it would still take quite a bit of work.

What if you could just draw the circle, cut it in half, and then apply a filter? If that worked, it would certainly save time and leave you with a perfect yin-yang symbol. After all, filters are applied with mathematical precision.

To see how easy it is to create the surprisingly complex shape of the yin-yang symbol, follow these steps:

1.

If you haven't done so already, start Illustrator and open a new file (File|New).

Set the Fill and Stroke to the default white and black, respectively. You can do this by clicking on the Default Fill and Stroke icon below and to the left of the Fill and Stroke icons in the Toolbar. Alternatively, you can press the "D" key. Then select the Ellipse tool and, while holding down the Shift key, draw a circle. Remember that holding down the Shift key restricts the elliptical shape to a circle.

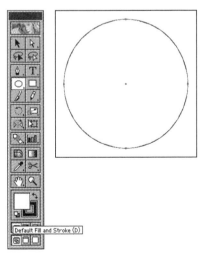

2.

Select the Scissors tool and cut the circle in two. You can do this by clicking on the top and bottom points on the circle. Try to get as close to the actual points as you can. You may want to zoom in first, using the Zoom tool, to help you place the Scissors tool right on top of the points.

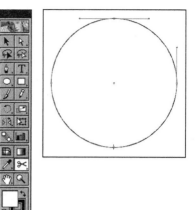

3.

With the circle cut in two, you can now join the two halves. I don't mean to reconnect the two halves, though. Instead, I want to join the ends of the new shapes to each other. To do so, select one half of the circle using the Selection tool and choose Object|Path|Join. This will join the curve, created by bisecting the circle, into a semicircular shape. Then repeat the process on the other half. You should now have two semicircles butted up against each other.

It's time to apply the filter.

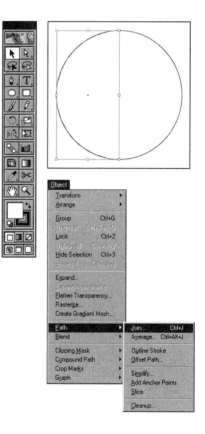

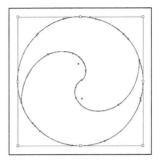

4.

The Twirl filter takes an object and twirls it. This can be used to create many wonderful shapes, and I encourage you to explore its power beyond its application in this project. You can, for example, apply it to type to create wild effects. Note that you'll have to create outlines from your type (with the type selected, choose Type|Create Outlines) first.

The Twirl filter twirls a shape, or shapes, around a center point. Because we have two shapes, we can twirl them around the collective center point of both. This will give us the effect of a yin-yang symbol. To create the yin-yang shape, select both halves of the circle using the Selection tool and choose Filter|Distort|Twirl. In the Twirl dialog box, enter "240" for the degrees of the twirl.

Wow! It's just like magic. The two shapes have twirled about each other to form the basic yin-yang symbol. A few steps are still needed to complete the shape, though.

5.

Choose the Selection tool and deselect the two shapes by clicking away from them. Then select just one of the shapes by clicking on it. You can change that shape's fill to black by clicking on the Fill icon in the Toolbar and then clicking on the black swatch in the Color palette. You'll now have two intertwined shapes, one in black and one in white.

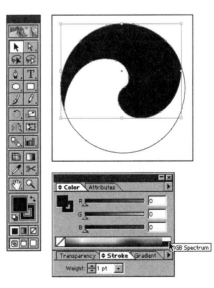

6.

We're still not finished, because the yin-yang symbol has a circular shape within each of the two halves. This small circle is easy to create now that the main shapes have been drawn. Select the Ellipse tool and draw a circle by clicking and dragging while holding down the Shift key. This shape will be drawn in black, because the fill color was just set to black in Step 5.

Move the circle into place in the white shape.

7.

Create a second circle by choosing Edit|Copy and then Edit|Paste In Front. You must change the Fill and Stroke of the new shape to white. You can do so by pressing "D" to set the default white fill and black stroke and then by setting the stroke to white. Move this second circle into place by holding down the Shift key and pressing the Arrow key that corresponds to the direction you want to move the circle.

That's it! Not bad for a couple of mouse clicks. If you want to see how complex this mathematical shape really is, try drawing it freehand using the Pen tool. Doing so will give you an appreciation for Illustrator's built-in filters.

Plenty of other filters are available in Illustrator. I encourage you to draw a couple of shapes and apply the different filters to them to see what effect they have on the shapes. You may be surprised at the results.

Project 2: Apply Bitmap Effects

Along with the ability to apply filters to vector-based objects created in Illustrator, you can also apply effects to bitmap images. You now have the same power over bitmap images in Illustrator as you would in Photoshop. You can apply blurs, sharpen a placed photograph, and more.

This next project will introduce you to the application of artistic effects to a placed photograph. You may not believe that it's possible to create a painterly effect in a vector-based drawing program such as Illustrator, but you can and the results can be stunning.

Create a Painterly Effect

Until recently, you needed to have access to a photo-editing program such as Photoshop to be able to create painterly effects. This is no longer true. Illustrator has the capability of adding many bitmap effects to your images. You can add textures, apply brushstrokes, and even give your images the look of a hand-painted masterpiece . . . all in Illustrator!

In this project, I'll show you how to apply different bitmap effects to a photograph. You'll also learn how to combine two layers with different effects to create a whole new image. If there's anything more fun than applying an effect, it's applying several effects to a single image to come up with a totally different result.

1.

To get started, open a new file and then choose File|Place. Browse to a folder that contains a scanned photograph you want to use. I will use a photograph of a tree in full spring bloom.

2.

Open the Link palette by choosing Window| View Links. Bring up the palette options menu by clicking on the small black arrow icon in the upper-right corner of the palette, and then choose Embed Image to embed the photograph.

3.

Because we are applying two separate effects and combining them, we need two separate layers with the same photograph on each.

Bring up the Layers palette by choosing Window|Show Layers. Then copy the original layer by dragging and dropping the layer containing the photograph onto the Create New Layer icon at the bottom of the Layers palette.

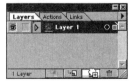

4.

To make it easier to work on Layer 1, turn off the visibility of the new layer by clicking on its Visibility Toggle icon in the Layers palette. Doing so means that we will be able to see any changes we make to the underlying layer.

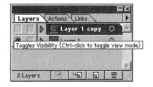

5.

Make the bottommost layer active by clicking on its name in the Layers palette. Then choose the embedded photograph by clicking on it with the Selection tool. Apply the Rough Pastels effect by choosing Effects|Artistic|Rough Pastels. In the Rough Pastels dialog box, set the Texture to Canvas, the Light Direction to Top Left, and the Scaling and Relief to 100% and 20, respectively.

I've set the Stroke Length and Stroke Detail to 6 and 4, respectively, but you may want to experiment with these settings depending on the photograph you're working with. The effect you want is that of a drawing created with large, rough pastels. You still want to see some detail, though.

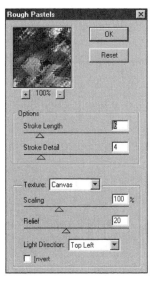

6.

To ensure that no further changes will be made to the Rough Pastels layer, you can lock the layer by clicking on its Lock Toggle icon in the Layers palette.

7.

It's time to work on the second layer. To do so, we'll need to activate it and turn its visibility back on.

Activate the second layer by clicking on its name in the Layers palette. Then turn its visibility back on by clicking on the Visibility Toggle icon in the Layers palette.

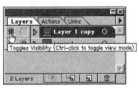

8.

The final effect I want is that of a pen and ink drawing with pastel coloring. To get the pen and ink effect, apply the Graphic Pen effect.

With the second layer active and visible, select the embedded photograph that was copied onto it earlier using the Selection tool. With the Photograph selected, apply the Graphic Pen effect by choosing Effect|Sketch|Graphic Pen.

In the Graphic Pen dialog box, I set the Stroke Length to 15, the Light/Dark Balance to 50, and the Stroke Direction to Right Diag. Feel free to experiment to get a particular effect if you don't like my settings.

9.

Now the top layer (the one with the Graphic Pen effect) is hiding the bottom layer (the one with the Rough Pastels effect). You could, of course, simply change the Transparency setting for the top layer to allow the bottom layer to show through. A better effect can be achieved by blending the two layers.

With the top layer still active, choose Window|Show Transparency to bring up the Transparency palette. Then set the Blend Mode to Soft Light. That's it.

10.

You can try this effect, and play around with different settings, on any scanned photograph or a photograph taken with a digital camera. In fact, you might want to try this same effect on a portrait. Something like this makes a great gift.

Project 3: Use Third-Party Filters

Even Illustrator, as powerful as it is and with its included filters and effects, can't do everything. This leaves room for third-party developers to create filters, known as plug-ins, that can extend the power of Illustrator.

Several plug-in filters are available from different companies including Hot Door, Metacreations (now available through Corel), and others. The filter I'm going to demonstrate here is called FILTERiT, available from Nakae Software; you can find it on the Internet at **www.cvalley.com**.

Note that FILTERiT, at the time this book was written, was available only for the Mac.

FILTERiT is easy to install. Simply run the install program, which will add the FILTERiT folder to the plug-in folder along with your other Illustrator filters.

Many different filters are available after you install FILTERiT. Many of these, including the Lens tool, are available as icons in the Toolbar. I will use the Lens tool to create an illustration of a golf ball. Although this would be possible to create without the benefit of the Lens tool, it would certainly be more time consuming than the method I describe here.

Create a Realistic Golf Ball

If you'd like to follow along with this project, you can download a demo copy of the filter from **www.cvalley.com**.

1.

Select the Ellipse tool and, while holding down the Shift key, draw a circle. You want the circle to be fairly small since we're going to create an array of them. In fact, we'll use 12 circles across and 12 circles down to create a large area filled with small circles.

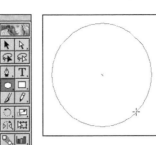

2.

Select the Gradient tool, set the Type to Radial, and fill the circle with a gradient by clicking and dragging the Gradient tool from the lower right towards, and beyond, the upper-left edge of the circle.

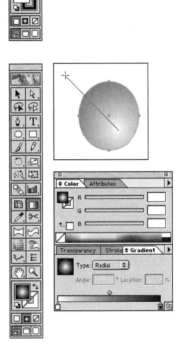

3.

Again, we're going to need many small circles...144, to be exact. The best way to create them all is to copy the first one and move it to the right, using the Shift key and the Right Arrow key. Note that I'm moving the copied circle to the right since I placed the first one in the upper-left corner of the artboard.

After copying the first circle, choose both circles using the Selection tool and paste them in front. Use the Shift key and the Arrow key to move these copies to the right, as well. You should now have four circles. Copy and Paste In Front of this group and move it to the right and repeat this step once more so that you have a row of 12 small, gradient-filled circles.

4.

Now that you have a row of 12 circles, you can copy and paste that row to make 12 rows of gradient-filled circles. This array of circles will become the dimples in the golf ball.

To create the 11 additional rows, simply copy the first row, after choosing all of the circles using the Selection tool, and then choose Edit|Copy and Edit|Paste In Front to create another row. Move this row below the first row by holding down the Shift key and tapping the Down Arrow key a few times.

Repeat the process until you have 12 rows of 12 circles. This may seem like a lot of work, but the copying and pasting actually goes quite quickly and, before you know it, you'll have 144 gradient-filled circles.

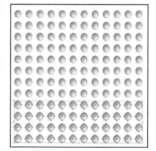

5.

As any avid golfer knows, golf balls have type on them. Usually this is the name of the manufacturer and a number that helps distinguish one ball from another when golfers play in foursomes and use golf balls from the same manufacturer.

To add type to your golf ball, create a new layer by clicking on the Create New Layer icon at the bottom of the Layers palette and add the text using the Type tool. Stretch the type so that it takes up a fairly large portion of the illustration.

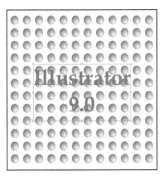

6.

Many effects and filters, including the FILTERiT Lens tool, will not process type. The solution, of course, is to convert the type to outlines.

To convert any type to outlines in Illustrator, simply select the type using the Selection tool and choose Type|Create Outlines. This will convert the type to vector-based objects that you can manipulate with all of the tool, filters, and effects available in Illustrator. Be aware, though, that this removes the ability to edit the type.

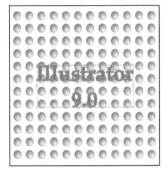

7.

With the dimples and the type in place, it's time to apply the FILTERiT Lens tool. You must select all of the objects you want to apply the effect to. To do so, drag a marquee around them using the Selection tool. Then select the FILTERiT Lens tool. This will bring up the FILTERiT Lens dialog box.

In the dialog box, I selected the Fisheye Lens, set the Thickness to 100%, and set both the Area Width and Area Height to 500 points. I arrived at this number by experimenting with the settings a couple of times, but I could just as easily have turned on the Grids or the Rulers to help me choose an accurate setting.

Don't worry if the filter doesn't encompass all of the dimples. You'll have some overlap in the corners. This is easy to rectify, though.

8.

To remove the extra dimples in the corners, simply select each in turn, using the Selection tool, and press the Delete key. This will leave you with a spherical series of dimples with spherical type in the center.

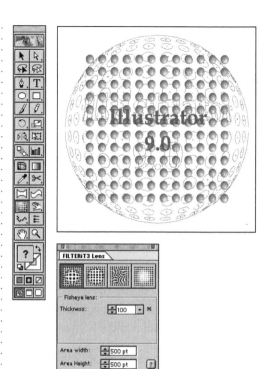

9.

To finish the golf ball, you'll need to add another gradient-filled circle as a covering. The new circle should be the same size as the area containing the dimples.

To create the new circle, add another layer and draw the circle using the Ellipse tool. Remember to hold down the Shift key to get a perfect circle. Drag the layer containing the cover below the dimples and type layers.

If you need to resize the new circle so that it matches the dimples, choose the circle using the Selection tool and drag out the corners of the bounding box until the circle matches up with the dimples.

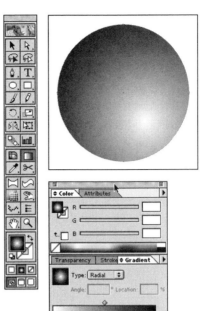

10.

To finalize the illustration, you need to add a gradient to the covering. It may already have a gradient due to the settings from the previous steps, but the gradient needs to be adjusted.

To draw the final gradient, select the Gradient tool and place the cursor near the upper left of the circle. Click and drag the cursor well below the lower right of the golf ball.

The end result should be a fairly realistic illustration of a golf ball.

Many more tools are available in the FILTERiT collection. There are also, as mentioned at the beginning of this project, several other good plug-ins available for you to explore. Most companies that create these tools have downloadable demos available from their respective Web sites.

Project 4: Use Photo Crosshatching Techniques

One of the most unusual filters available in Illustrator is the Photo Crosshatch filter. It has many mysterious-sounding settings and does not appear to give you the promised effect.

Create a Hatching Effect from a Photograph

Although this next project may not clear up all of the mysteries, it will show you how to apply the Photo Crosshatch filter with good results. To find out how to create a crosshatch effect from a photograph, follow these steps.

1.

To get started, open a photograph in Illustrator. You can use a .psd file that was scanned into Photoshop or open a file of a photograph that you took with a digital camera. You should use a photograph that has a good tonal range, since this is what the filter bases its hatching effect on. And because the filter uses tonal ranges and not colors, you might want to consider converting the photograph to grayscale using Photoshop.

If you placed the photograph into Illustrator instead of opening it, you will have to embed the file using the Links palette since the filter will not operate on a placed image.

2.

We will use the crosshatch filter on two layers to create a deeper effect. You can, of course, create more layers and add the effect to all of them to get a rich effect. Be aware, though, that this takes up a lot of memory; adding too many layers will complicate the final result visually.

I'll use the lower layer as the shadow layer. That is, I'll adjust the Photo Crosshatch settings to draw in the shadow areas of the lower layer. In the upper layer, I'll adjust the settings of the Photo Crosshatch filter to draw in the midtones and highlight areas.

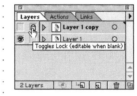

3.

So that we can work on the original layer without disturbing the new upper layer, we will lock the upper layer and toggle off its visibility.

4.

Activate the lower layer by clicking on its name in the Layers palette and choose the photograph using the Selection tool.

5.

Choose Filter|Pen and Ink|Photo Crosshatch to open the Photo Crosshatch dialog box.

You can safely ignore most of the settings for now, but some do need to be set. Set the Thickness to 0.4 pt. This sets the thickness of the lines that will be drawn. I want thicker lines for the shadows. I'll adjust this to a lower value for the upper layer. Set the Max. Line Length to 24 pt. I want shorter lines for the shadows. I'll adjust this to a higher value for the upper layer. Set the Hatch Layers to 2. Leave the gradient bar set towards the left so that the filter works on the shadow areas of the photograph.

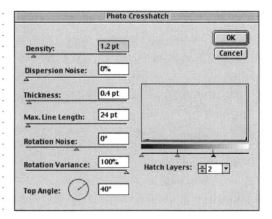

6.

Examine the results of the filter's application. You should see hatch marks in the shadow, or darker, areas of your image. If the results are not satisfactory, choose Edit|Undo and reapply the filter after resetting some of the values.

7.

Lock the lower layer now that it's done. Unlock the upper layer and toggle its visibility so that you can apply the Photo Crosshatch to it. Make the upper layer active by clicking on its name in the Layers palette, and finally, choose the photograph using the Selection tool.

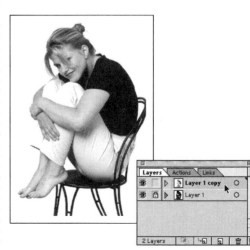

8.

It's time to apply the Photo Crosshatch filter to the upper layer. This time, I'll apply the filter to affect the brighter areas of the photograph.

This time, I'll change the Thickness to 0.2 pt. to use a thinner line for the highlights and midtones. I'll also set the Max. Line Length to 48 pt. to get longer lines. Finally, I'll drag the sliders for the gradient over to the right. I won't go all the way to the right, though, as that would fill the white areas of this particular photograph.

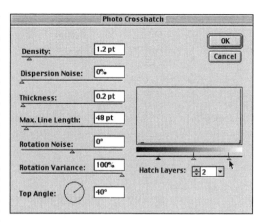

9.

Click on OK to apply the filter and then click away from the image with the Selection tool to deselect everything. You should have a nice crosshatched image that appears similar to something you'd have to work on for hours using pen and ink to achieve.

Again, if the results are not what you expected, choose Edit|Undo and apply the filter again after changing some of the settings. Use my values in this exercise as a starting point.

10.

To add a touch of interest to the final image, you can change the color of the stroke on the crosshatches. To do so, select all of the cross-hatches on the upper layer. This should be easy to do with the lower layer still locked. Simply drag a marquee around the image using the Selection tool. Next, change the stroke color. I changed the stroke on the upper layer to a bright red by clicking on the Stroke icon in the Toolbar and changing the color in the Color palette.

You can start out using more layers and then change the colors of the stroke on each layer. No doubt you'll come up with your own application of this powerful and what should now be a less-mysterious filter.

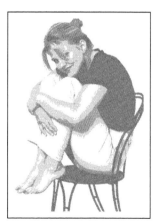

Chapter 14
An Interface for
a Web Site

Creating Web-Site Interfaces

People are always looking for new ideas for their Web site interfaces. The following projects will demonstrate how to create interfaces you can use on your own Web site and on sites you may create for others. Specifically, we demonstrate how to create a tabbed interface, a metallic navigational bar, and a remote-style interface.

Project 1: A Tabbed Interface

Tabbed interfaces are all the rage. Many large business sites use the tabbed metaphor to enable their customers to navigate their Web sites.

The idea is elegant and fairly easy to implement. You need to make a couple of decisions before you get started, though. You need to decide if the interface should run horizontally along the top of the Web pages or vertically along the side. You also should decide, up front, how many tabs you need, since making a change to this design may be more time intensive than with other designs. And you should decide how to give your visitors a visual clue as to where they are in the context of your site.

In this project, I show you how to create a horizontal layout using five tabs. I use a color for the tab representing the current page and gray for the other tabs (of course, you'll see the interface being developed in shades of gray since this book was printed in black and white). This should give visitors a visual clue that tells them where they are in the site. If you decide to use this metaphor, you could also add some text below the tabs as a header that gives your visitors even more information.

Plan the Layout

As I said earlier, I am creating a horizontal tabbed interface. You can, of course, use many of the same methods presented in the following project to create a similar tabbed interface with a different number of buttons or a vertical tabbed interface. It shouldn't be too difficult to translate the steps to produce the effect you want.

Before you get started, you should open a new image. To help you with the planning and sizing of the elements that make up the tabbed interface, set the Width to 600 points and the Height to 400 points in the Artboard Size and set the Color Mode to RGB, which is the color mode used for onscreen images such as those displayed on a Web page. Setting the artboard to 600×400 points will approximate the average browser display size and will give you the opportunity to see what the final image will look like when it's viewed.

As easy as it is to resize objects in Illustrator, you need to decide ahead of time how many tabs you need, since resetting the size of the tabs may distort them somewhat.

Create the Tabs

With the major decisions out of the way, it's time to create the tabs. To create tabs for your Web page interface, follow these steps:

New Document

Name: Tabbed Interface   OK

Cancel

Color Mode
○ CMYK Color
● RGB Color

Artboard Size
Width: 600 pt
Height: 400 pt

1.

To get started, select the Rounded Rectangle tool and draw a rounded rectangle. This will be the basis for the tab shape.

2.

Adding a rectangle will square off the bottom edges of the tab. This will give the appearance of the tab being part of the Web page. With several tabs spread along in a row, they will appear as several tabbed pages, one behind the next.

To draw the rectangle, select the Rectangle tool, place the cursor along the left edge of the rounded rectangle from Step 1, and click and drag towards the right edge of the rounded rectangle. You may find it helpful if you zoom in using the Zoom tool. This can make exact placement a lot easier.

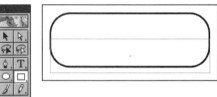

3.

The two shapes—the rounded rectangle and the rectangle—must be combined into a single shape. This is easily done by selecting the two shapes using the Selection tool, and then clicking on the Unite icon under the Combine options in the Pathfinder palette (choose Window|Show Pathfinder).

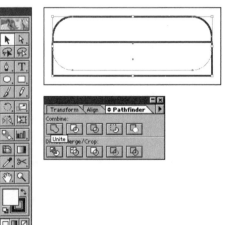

4.

The bottom of the new shape must be removed. This can easily be done with a couple of "cuts" with the Scissors tool. Select the tool and cut the object at both lower corners. Then, select the bottom line using the Selection tool and press the Delete key to remove the bottom line from the object.

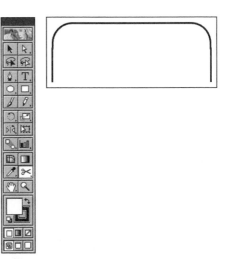

5.

It's time to add a line to the object—two lines actually, one at each end of the object. Before you draw the first line, choose the Selection tool and click anywhere in the artboard to deselect the object.

Select the Pen tool and place it at the end of the line at the left side of the object. Click and release the mouse. Now move the mouse to the left and, while holding the Shift key, click again to complete the line. Holding down the Shift key ensures that the line will be drawn horizontally.

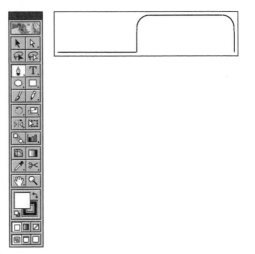

6.

Repeat the process from Step 5, but draw the line to the right of the object and make it longer. Make sure that you deselect the object using the Selection tool before you begin drawing the second line.

Notice that I haven't been too specific about the length of the lines. It doesn't matter about length at this point, because it is a simple matter to lengthen or shorten lines as necessary.

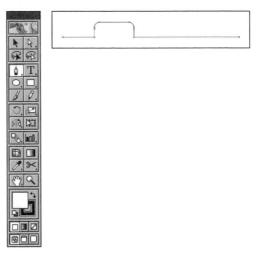

7.

With the first tab drawn, it's time to move it into place so it can be adjusted. Choose the object using the Selection tool and move it fairly close to the left side of the artboard. Remember that you're using the artboard in order to see how the final artwork will appear in a Web browser.

You may notice that I let the left line overlap the artboard. This doesn't matter as much as placing the tab correctly. I want some space between the side of the browser (in this case, the artboard) and the tab itself. The lines will, of course, need to be adjusted.

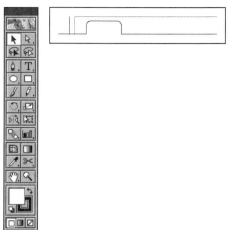

8.

Adjusting the length of the lines is simple with a little trick. You need to select just the point at the end of the line. This is a simple matter with the help of the Direct Selection tool. Select the tool and draw a rectangle around the leftmost point of the left line that extends from the tab object. With the point selected, you can shorten or lengthen the line using the cursor keys to move the point to the left or right (the left arrow and the right arrow keys, respectively). Holding down the Shift key at the same time will move the point 10 pixels at a time, thereby speeding up the process.

Use the arrow keys to shorten and lengthen the two lines so that they reach almost to the ends of the artboard.

9.

It's time to make the second tab. The easiest way to do this is to copy the first. Choose the object using the Selection tool and then choose Edit|Copy and Edit|Paste In Back. This will copy the tab object, paste it behind the original, and leave the copy selected. Now hold down the Shift key and use the arrow key to move it below the original and to the right. You need to move it below the original tab so you can correct the line lengths of the copy as you did with the original tab in Step 8.

10.

Repeat Step 9 as many times as necessary to get the number of tabs you need for your Web page interface. I made five tabbed objects in all.

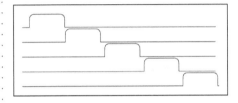

11.

With everything lined up, you can move the tabs into place so they form one long row. Simply choose each, using the Selection tool, and move them into place. Because you moved the tabs after copying and pasting them, you can move them back the same way and line them up precisely.

12.

Your interface needs some text labels on the tabs to help visitors find their way around. Create a new layer by clicking on the Create New Layer icon in the Layers palette. Having done so, you can arrange the tab objects without disturbing the type. Select the Type tool, click on the first tab, and enter some text. Generally this should be the tab that directs visitors to the home page. I used 14 point Verdana for the type and added text for all five tabs.

| Home | Books | Tutorials | Reviews | Links |

13.

For this interface, I want to color the current tab and leave the others gray. To color the first tab, choose it with the Selection tool and then set the Fill color. I set the color to a bright cyan by sliding the Red slider in the Color palette to 0 while leaving the Green and Blue set to 255.

| Home | Books | Tutorials | Reviews | Links |

14.

Color the second tab a light gray by choosing it with the Selection tool and setting the Red, Green, and Blue sliders to 200 in the Color palette. To set the remaining tabs to the same gray, select each in turn (use the Shift key to select more than one object at a time) and then click on the second tab using the Eyedropper tool. This will copy the fill and stroke to the selected objects.

| Home | Books | Tutorials | Reviews | Links |

15.

I want each tab to act as part of a hotlink on an image map. If I were to select any one tab, though, I would select the entire object along with the lines. This would cause the objects to overlap. To solve this, I'll create a new layer between the tab object layer and the type layer and I'll create a rectangle over each tab on this new layer. These can then be selected and used as part of an image map. Create a new layer between the tabs and the type and create five rectangles using the Rectangle tool.

With all rectangles created, select each in turn, and in the Attributes palette set the Image Map option to Rectangle and enter a name that corresponds to the tab. Once you've named them, you can hide each tab by assigning a fill and stroke of None to each. This will ensure the image map works correctly, while hiding the rectangles you've created as hot spots.

16.

You can save the objects in several ways and then use them all together on a Web page. Because they're small and I like to keep the HTML simple, I'll save each set as one graphic. This means that I'll save the file with the Home tab colored and the others grayed out. I'll then color the second tab, gray out the Home tab, and save it as Books. I'll continue until I have five separate files, each with one tab colored and the others grayed out. I'll load the appropriate graphic on the five different pages.

To save the file and have it create the HTML file, I'll export the graphic as a JPEG. In the JPEG Options dialog box, I'll set the option for Anti Alias and, more important, I'll set the option for Imagemap. This will write out the JPEG file and save the HTML for the image map.

17.

It's time to color the second tab and gray out the Home tab. To do so, I'll select the Books tab and then, using the Eyedropper tool, click on the Home tab to copy the color from it to the Books tab.

With the Books tab colored, I'll gray out the Home tab by selecting it and clicking on one of the gray tabs with the Eyedropper tool.

18.

To export the Books tab, follow the same basic process outlined in Step 16 to export the new graphic along with the associated HTML image map file.

19.

Repeat Steps 16 through 18 as necessary until all tabs have been colored and all of the separate graphics have been saved. When all files have been saved and exported as image maps, you can easily double-click on one of the HTML files to test it in your favorite Web browser.

The beauty of this approach to creating an interface is that the HTML files are started for you. All you have to do is add the content.

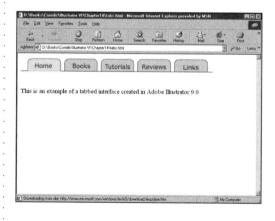

Project 2: A Metallic Navigational Bar

Another popular interface is the metallic navigational bar. This is fairly easy to create in Illustrator using some basic shapes, a couple of gradients, and some type.

Plan the Interface

Again, you should plan ahead a little. You should set up the artboard to reflect the size of a common browser; I used 600 points for the width and 400 points for the height. Remember that the settings are mainly used as guidelines so you can create your graphics at a good size. I also set the Color Mode to RGB, since this is what computer screens use.

Create the Interface

With the initial setup done, you can get started creating the interface. The end result should resemble a metallic bar with buttons etched into it. To create this interface, follow these steps:

1.

To get started, create an ellipse using the Ellipse tool. This will be one side of the navigational bar.

2.

Choose Edit|Copy and then Edit|Paste In Front to create a second ellipse on top of the first. Move this to the right of the artboard.

3.

Select the Rectangle tool and draw a rectangle between the two ellipses. Combine all three shapes by using the Selection tool and clicking on the Unite icon under the Combine options in the Pathfinder palette. This finishes the shape of the navigational bar.

4.

Choose the shape using the Selection tool. Select the Gradient tool and click on the small swatch in the Gradient palette to apply the gradient to the object.

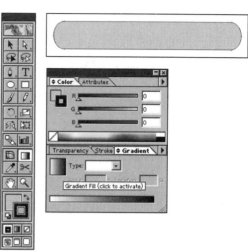

5.

To create the metallic look, the gradient needs to be edited. First, change the Angle to 270 degrees and set the Type to Linear. This causes the gradient to change gradually from white to black from the top of the object to the bottom.

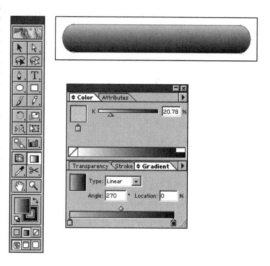

6.

Click on the rightmost slider at the bottom of the Gradient palette and change the color from white to a pale gray.

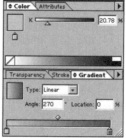

7.

Click below the gradient between the sliders to add another slider. With the new slider created, change its color to white. Then add more sliders using various shades of gray to create a metallic effect.

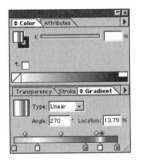

You can move the diamond icons above the sliders to change how the shades interact. For example, you can move them closer together to create a highlight or shadow line.

You should now have a metallic-looking bar with rounded ends complete with highlights and shadows. The effect you want is that of a 3D metal bar.

8.

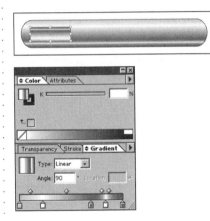

Use the Rectangle tool to create a rectangular shape. Create it on a new layer to keep it separate from the main shape.

Note that the shape is created using the same gradient as the main shape. To get the look of a shape that's been etched into the metal, you need to reverse the angle. To do so, simply change the Angle in the Gradient palette from 270 degrees to 90 degrees.

9.

Create three copies of the rectangle by copying and pasting in front, so that the resulting interface has four buttons. Note that although I'm creating a bar with four buttons, you can create as many as are needed for your interface.

10.

Select the Type tool and add some type over each rectangle. These will serve as buttons on the interface.

11.

Choose each rectangle, using the Selection tool, and make it a hotlink area in an image map by naming it and setting the Image Map to Rectangle in the Attributes palette.

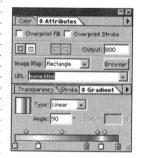

12.

Export the graphic as a JPEG; then, in the JPEG Options dialog box, set the Anti-Alias and Imagemap options. This will create the HTML for your metallic navigational bar.

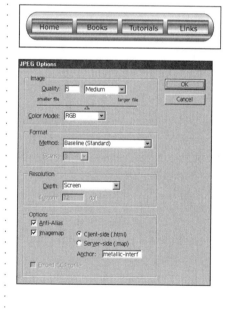

Project 3: A Remote-Style Interface

Many unique interfaces are used throughout the Web, and many Web sites are intended to showcase the digital artists' talents with the programs they use. But what do you do if you're not familiar enough with the software to create such stunning designs? Simple! You use a familiar design that's easy to create yet cool enough to use on your Web site. Follow these steps to create a remote-style interface. I chose this style because remote controls are ubiquitous and easy to draw using shapes and lines. That said, let's get started.

Plan the Interface

Again, you should plan ahead. You should set up the artboard to reflect the size of a common browser; I am using 600 points for the width and 400 points for the height. Remember that the settings are used mainly as guidelines so you can create your graphics at a good size. I also set the Color Mode to RGB since this is what computer screens use.

Create the Interface

With the initial setup done, you can start creating the interface. The result should resemble a television or VHS remote control. I've added a text-based logo to the design, which features easy-to-create buttons. Feel free to add your own logo if you've created one while working through this book, or simply add your own initials.

1.

First select the Ellipse tool and create an ellipse. It should be fairly long and narrow, but
not too narrow. This will be the top of the remote shape. Don't worry about the stroke and
fill colors; you can use the default colors or
any others you like, and then you can easily
reset them after the shape is complete.

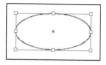

2.

Select the ellipse you've just created and choose
Edit|Copy and then Edit|Paste In Front to paste
a copy of the ellipse directly in front of the original shape.

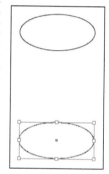

While holding down the Shift+Control (or
Shift+Command on a Mac) keys, press the
down arrow key several times to place the copied ellipse below the original one. I did this
about 18 or 19 times to move the copied ellipse almost to the bottom of the artboard.

3.

Select the Rectangle tool and draw a rectangle
that joins the two ellipses. You may want to
zoom in first using the Zoom tool to get the
placement just right. You should start the rectangle at the middle point of one of the ellipses
and end it at the opposite point of the other
ellipse.

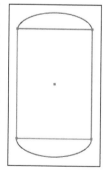

When you're done, you should have two ellipses joined by a rectangle.

4.

All three shapes must be combined to create the final remote-control shape. To combine the shapes, choose all three using the Selection tool and then click on the Unite icon in the Pathfinder palette. If this palette is not visible, choose Window|Show Pathfinder.

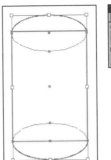

5.

It would be nice to add some depth to the remote control; to do so, you need two copies of the shape. One will be the actual remote control, and the other will be used to create a highlight and shadow to give the appearance of depth.

To make a second copy to be used as the highlight/shadow, choose Object|Path|Offset Path. This will create a new copy of the shape—one that will be larger than the first. I've chosen to make the offset 10 points larger. If the units listed in the Offset dialog box are not "pt", don't worry: You can simply type "pt" to get the same results.

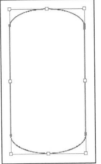

6.

The shape you just created will be selected, and you can now change the default stroke and fill to the colors the final interface should be. I chose a dark blue for the fill and set the stroke to none. You, of course, can choose any color you want.

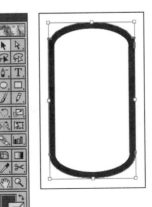

7.

The new, larger shape will be still be selected; you should temporarily lock it so you can manipulate the smaller shape without selecting the new one. To lock the selected shape, choose Object|Lock.

8.

To start creating the highlight/shadow, it is necessary to cut the inner shape into two parts. To do so, select the Scissors tool and cut the shape at the lower-left and upper-right corners. This will leave you with two shapes that you can manipulate separately.

You may want to zoom in using the Zoom tool to help you make accurate cuts. You should cut the lines where you see the control points. Depending on your color choices and the zoom level, it may be hard to see any changes. You will, though, have two separate shapes to work with.

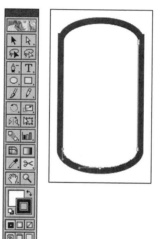

9.

Choose the upper shape using the Selection tool and change the stroke to white and the fill to none. In the Stroke palette, set the Weight to 8 pts. This white line will become the highlight of the remote control. If you don't see this palette, choose Window|Show Stroke.

10.

Using the Selection tool, select the lower shape and set the stroke to black and the fill to none. Then set the stroke weight to 8 pts. in the Stroke palette. This line will become the shadow of the remote control.

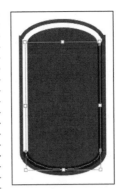

11.

Choose both the white and black lines using the Selection tool. Remember that you can se-lect multiple objects by holding down the Shift key as you select them.

To soften the highlight/shadow, you can ap-ply a blur effect. To do so, choose Effect|Blur| Gaussian Blur. I set the blur radius to 3.0 pix-els. You can experiment with different values to see different effects. Simply undo the effect each time using Edit|Undo until you're happy with the outcome. At this point, you should have the final remote control shape. All it needs is a logo and some buttons.

12.

Before you add the letters of your logo, you might want to create a shape to hold them and help them stand out. I created a 3D-spherical effect by adding a circle and filling it with a gradient. You can create the same effect by drawing a circle with the Ellipse tool. To create a perfect circle, hold down the Shift key while dragging the tool.

With the circle created, fill it with a radial gradient. This will give the effect of a 3D-spherical shape and will complement the 3D remote control. To create the gradient fill, set the fill style to Gradient and set the colors in the Gradient dialog box. Then click and drag the Gradient tool from near the upper-left of the circle towards the lower-right. I set the colors of the gradient to range from white to a light blue, but you can choose something that will match the color scheme you've chosen for your Web site.

13.

Add some text to the logo using the Type tool. Don't worry about the font size because you will need to resize the type manually to fit the logo. After typing in your letters, choose them using the Selection tool, move them into place, and resize them to fit in the space. I used the Myriad font for my "GD" for GrafX Design.

By default, type is added with a black fill and no stroke. To create the effect of indented type, you should swap the fill and stroke so that the letters are outlined in black. To complete the effect, you need another copy of the same type on top of the original. The new copy should be stroked with white and offset slightly below and to the right of the original. To create the second copy, choose Edit|Copy and then Edit|Paste In Front; to color it, set the stroke to white. Finally, move the copy down and to the right by tapping the down arrow and then the right arrow keys once each.

14.

To create a shape that will hold the buttons, draw a rounded rectangle shape using the Rounded Rectangle tool. Draw the shape and move it into position along the left side of the remote control. I filled the shape with black, but you may choose any color that suits your needs.

You can make the shape stand out more by adding an offset copy, filled with white, behind the original shape. You can do so by choosing the shape with the Selection tool and choosing Edit|Copy and then Edit|Paste In Back. Move the copy to the right and down by tapping on the down and right arrow keys a couple of times.

15.

Use the Rectangle tool to add some rectangular-shaped buttons to the remote control. I used a simple light blue to complement the color I used for the logo.

You can draw all the button shapes by hand or draw one and then copy it using Edit|Copy and Edit|Paste. This method creates each button with the same dimensions. If you choose Paste In Front, it's a simple matter to line up the buttons as well. Simply use the arrow keys to move each button into position.

16.

Use the Type tool to add text to your buttons. You can use the same font as you used for your logo. Use the Selection tool to place and size your text as needed. I've added five buttons to my remote control, but you can add as many or as few as you need for your site.

17.

You may have noticed that offsetting the path at the beginning of this project has caused a small deformation of the overall shape. This is easily fixed. To fix the shape caused by the Offset command, unlock the main shape by choosing Objects|Unlock All. Then, using the Direct Selection tool, click and drag the control points until they line up.

At this point, you can add other shapes and buttons to give the remote control a unique look and feel. Whatever you do, have fun and play around with Illustrator's tools and the techniques you've learned in this book.

Index

If you like this book, you'll love these...

FLASH™ 5 F/X AND DESIGN

Bill Sanders
ISBN: 1-57610-816-3
416 pages with CD-ROM • $49.99 U.S. • $74.99 CANADA

Flash™ 5 f/x and Design helps the intermediate to advanced Flash user create aesthetically pleasing, interactive web sites. Animation; tweening; using the timeline; coordinating sounds, shape, color, scenes, movement, and sequences; scripting actions; and interfaces are covered. Readers gain an understanding of Flash's underlying conceptual framework for creating movies. The CD-ROM includes more than 50 projects in both FLA and SWF files.

LOOKING GOOD ON THE WEB

Daniel Gray
ISBN: 1-57610-508-3
224 pages • $29.99 U.S. • $43.99 CANADA

Written from the user's perspective, this book provides a comprehensive, non-technical introduction to Web design. You'll learn how to design and create friendly, easily navigable, award-winning Web sites that please clients and visitors alike.

PHOTOSHOP® 6 VISUAL INSIGHT

Ramona Pruitt and Joshua Pruitt
ISBN: 1-57610-747-7
416 pages • $29.99 U.S. • $44.99 CANADA

Learn the basic features of Photoshop®, including layering, masks, and paths, as well as intermediate functions, such as Web graphics, filters, and actions. This book teaches the most useful Photoshop techniques and allows readers to use these in real-world projects, such as repairing images, eliminating red eye, creating type effects, developing Web elements, and more.

ILLUSTRATOR® 9 F/X AND DESIGN

Sherry London
ISBN: 1-57610-750-7
560 pages with CD-ROM • $49.99 U.S. • $74.99 CANADA

Features new information and projects on styles and effects, how to integrate with Web products, and other enhanced features. Using real-world projects, readers learn firsthand how to create intricate illustrations and compositing techniques. Readers also learn how to work seamlessly between Illustrator® and Photoshop®.

The Coriolis Group, LLC   Telephone: 480.483.0192 • Toll-free: 800.410.0192 • In Canada: 905.477.0722 • www.coriolis.com
Coriolis books are also available at bookstores and computer stores nationwide.